leaf
Publishing

iPad

For Seniors

Welcome

The iPad is one of the most useful pieces of technology you can buy. Not only can you browse the internet with it, but you can make video calls to friends and family, take amazing photos, watch movies and TV shows, and even take part in a fitness class.

The best thing about the iPad, however, is that it's so easy to use. You can never do the wrong thing, as the Home screen is just a swipe of your finger away; and if you're ever unsure what to do, then you can simply ask Siri -- the iPad's digital assistant.

This fully updated book for 2021 is all about making sense of the iPad, even if you've never used one before. You'll learn about the very basics, how the built-in apps work, and how you can use an iPad to enrich and improve your life. Large images and step-by-step guides are used throughout to help you along the way.

As you become more familiar with the iPad and its apps, you might have specific questions that aren't covered in this book. If so, feel free to send me an email at tom@leafpublishing.co.uk, and I'll be happy to help.

Tom Rudderham
Author
tom@leafpublishing.co.uk

Credits:

Author: Tom Rudderham
Editor: Zeljko Jurancevic
Copy Editor: Caroline Denham

Published by:
Leaf Publishing LTD
www.leafpublishing.co.uk

ISBN:
9798688631111

Contents

Welcome

Setting Up

30
Set up Face ID
& Touch ID

The Basics

Accessories

Apps

Web & Communication

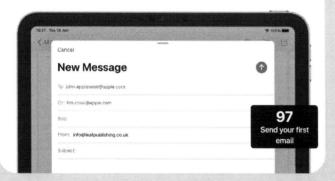

97
Send your first email

Maps, Notes, & Utilities

125
Explore the world in 3D

Camera & Photos

115
Learn how to take panoramic photos

Settings & Troubleshooting

153
Use Assistive Touch

Entertainment & news

Terminology

Wondering what all those words and phrases mean?

The iPad is a state of the art piece of equipment, so perhaps it's inevitable that talking about it involves using a wide-ranging assortment of words, phrases, and terminology. In this book, you're going to hear a lot about the iPad hardware, software, and features. Don't worry, each one of them will be explained as we go, so you'll never feel confused or get lost halfway through a paragraph. To get you started, here are a few of the words we will be using constantly throughout this book...

Whenever the word hardware is used, we're basically talking about the iPad in its physical form. The thing which you hold in your hand.

Think of software as a set of instructions for doing something on your iPad. These instructions might be millions of words long, and they were probably written by a large team of people. To most humans, it's utter gibberish. It looks something like this:

```
int main(int argc, char * argv[]) {
    @autoreleasepool {
        return UIApplicationMain( argc, argv, nil,
NSStringFromClass( [AVCamAppDelegate
class] ) );
    }
```

To a programmer who writes in Swift (Apple's programming language), this makes perfect sense. It's just a fraction of the code required to tell your iPad how to capture an image using its camera. The full piece of code is tens of thousands of lines long.

The word app is short for "application", and an application is a tool used to do something on your iPad. Let's say you want to take a photo on your iPad. To do this, you open the Camera app. If you want to look for something on the internet, then you need to open the Safari app. Keep telling yourself that an app is a tool, and you'll get the idea.

iPadOS

This is the name of the software which powers your iPad. It's one of the most complicated pieces of software ever created by man. It tells your iPad how to turn on, how to take a photo, how to browse the internet, how to scan your face when you want to unlock your iPad, plus so much more. It can also learn over time. iOS will learn about your habits, how you type to individual people, where you travel, what you look like and what you sound like. It uses all of this learning to help you type quicker, find photos quicker, and basically use your iPad in a more efficient manner.

You don't have to worry about security either, because all of this personal information is fully encrypted, and the really important stuff, like your voice and face information, never leaves your iPad.

When most people think of the word iOS, they imagine the home screen of their iPad. The place where all the icons are which let you open the internet browser or email application. You can think of it like that too, but really it's so much more.

Encryption

Think of encryption as a padlock for words, but instead of 0-9 on the padlock, it's A-Z, plus 0-9. The software on your iPad uses encryption all the time. Whenever you send a message to a friend, all the letters you type are scrambled up, sent to the other person, then de-scrambled on their device. The same goes for video calls you make using FaceTime, your credit cards details when you check out on the internet, and much more. Nearly everything you do on your iPad is encrypted, which is why even the FBI can't access your device without your password or biometric information.

App Store

Think of the App Store as a marketplace for apps. Some apps are free, others cost a few dollars/pounds/euros. Some apps look like they are free, but ask for a payment to do something (this is called an "In-App Purchase"). You can find the App Store on your iPad. It has a bright blue icon with an abstract "A" in the middle.

Download

The term "download" is used whenever something from the internet is transferred onto your iPad. It could be an app, a song, a photo, or even a document. So if you hear someone say "I downloaded a new app to my iPad", they're basically saying that they copied an app from the internet to their iPad.

Multitasking

A term to describe doing multiple things at once. When we talk about multitasking on the iPad, we usually mean opening and running two apps at once.

Terminology continuined

Browser

This is the term used to describe an app for navigating the internet. On the iPad, the "browser "is called Safari, but there are other browsers available to install from the App Store, such as Chrome, Firefox, and Microsoft Edge.

Restart

The word "restart" is used when something needs to be turned off, then back on again. Maybe your iPad needs to be restarted because it has stopped working, or similarly an app might need to be restarted.

Siri

Think of Siri as a virtual assistant that you can talk too. You can ask Siri what the weather is like, directions to somewhere, basic math questions, or even the answers to trivia.

Storage

Your iPad comes with a limited amount of space for storing photos, videos, apps, and other content. When you bought your iPad, you needed to choose how much storage it had available, and the more storage space you chose, the more expensive it was to buy.

Sleep

You can put your iPad to sleep by pressing the lock button on the top of the device. When it's asleep, it will still check for new messages, emails, and notifications, but the screen will be turned off, and it won't use much power. In sleep mode, your iPad can last for nearly a week on a full battery charge, while in normal use (when the screen is on), it's more like 10 hours.

Gigabyte / GB

This storage comes in gigabytes (AKA GB), with the most affordable iPad Pro coming with 128GB of storage, and the most expensive having 1,000GB.

To put that into context, you can typically save around 250 photos per gigabyte, or approximately 10 minutes of video.

Settings

You can heavily configure how your iPad notifies you of new messages, how bright the screen is, how loud the speakers are, and even how apps track your location. These configurations are called "settings', and to make any of these changes (plus much more), then you need to open the Settings app.

Gestures

When we talk about gestures on the iPad, we're referring to the use of your fingers to initiate an action. Let's say you want to zoom into a photo. The gesture to do this would be to place two fingers on the screen then move them apart.

Home

The "Home" screen is where you'll find all the apps installed on your iPad. It's the first place you see after unlocking your iPad, and every time you close an app, you'll return to the Home screen.

Attachments

If you receive an email that includes a photo, video, or document, then it is usually referred to as an attachment.

Icon

The small image that represents an app is usually referred too as an "icon". It's basically a small image that when tapped on, lets you open an app, or initiate an action.

Don't understand another term?

Feel free to email Tom, the author of this book at tom@leafpublishing.co.uk, and he'll be happy to explain any further terms or phrases that you're unsure about.

Things to keep in mind

The iPad is easier to use than you might think...

Whether you've bought a new iPad or been given one by a friend or family member, there are a few things to keep in mind.

You do everything with just your fingertip

When you want to open an app, make a picture bigger, or scroll through a page, all you need to do is tap on the screen with your fingertip. Touch screens work by detecting the static electricity from your finger, so you don't need to press hard to do anything. A light tap will work. Keep in mind that fingernails don't transmit static, only skin, so if you have long fingernails, try tapping with the soft part of your finger.

You can never do the wrong thing

You'll never break your iPad by opening the wrong app, or by tapping on the wrong button, so don't worry about making a mistake. Most apps have sensible names, so if you want to send a message, open the Messages app, and if you want to look at photos, tap on the Photos app.

If you're unsure about an app, feel free to open it anyway, you can always go back by swiping your finger from the very bottom of the screen to the top. If you have an regular iPad or iPad mini, then you can press the round button below the screen (called the Home button) to perform the same action.

You can talk to your iPad

Your iPad has a built-in assistant called Siri (covered in more detail later in this book). You can use Siri to do basic things like making a phone call, perform simple maths, set a reminder, or set a timer. To do this, press and hold the power button on your iPad, or the Home button below the screen, wait for a small circular graphic to appear, then say out-loud something like "call Joe", "remind me to take the dinner out of the over in 10 minutes", or "what's 15 times 30?". After a moment or two, Siri will perform your request.

The are two kinds of iPad

Regular iPad's and the iPad mini have a button beneath the screen. This is called the Home button, and you can press it to close an app. Neither the iPad Air or the iPad Pro have a Home button, so you close apps by swiping upwards from the bottom of the screen. They also have an easily recognisable notch at the top of the screen.

Don't worry which iPad you have, as apart from closing apps and opening Siri, they work in pretty much the same way.

iPad's come in many sizes

All iPad's work the same way, but to accomodate our individual needs and budgets, there are four sizes to choose from:

iPad mini

It has a 7.9 inch display, and weighs just 300 grams.

iPad

It has a 10.2 inch display, and weighs just 490 grams.

iPad Air, & iPad Pro

The Air has a 10.9 inch display, and weighs 458 grams. The Pro weighs a little bit more, at 474 grams.

iPad Pro

It has a 12.9 inch display, and weighs 641 grams.

iPad

The iPad represents everything *classic* about the iPad. It sits in the sweet spot between size and weight, and it has a 9.7-inch display - just like the original iPad. It also happens to be the cheapest iPad you can buy.

There's a reason why the iPad is more affordable than it's larger and smaller siblings: it lacks a display with support for the P3 colour gamut (which makes photos and colours appear to really "pop" off the screen), and it also lacks support for True Tone (which alters the white balance of the display to match the environment around you). The screen is also non-laminated, which means it sits further behind the glass than other iPads. Internally, the iPad comes with the A11 Bionic processor, and it's limited to 2GB of RAM.

To most people, these slightly-lower specifications won't make much difference. Apps will take a fraction of a second longer to open, Safari tabs might refresh more often, and photographs will appear a little more faded, but for its price, the iPad represents an excellent purchase for anyone looking for a basic iPad.

Pros:

- Affordable.
- The "classic" iPad size.
- Full-size keyboard in landscape orientation.

Cons:

- Only supports the first-generation Apple Pencil.
- No face recognition.
- No ultra-wide camera.
- Two speakers, rather than four.
- The 9.7-inch display can be cramped when using productivity apps.

iPad mini

If you love everything about the iPad Air, but want an iPad that's much smaller and easier to carry, then the iPad mini is the perfect choice.

It's basically an iPad Air shrunk down, so you still get a beautiful Retina display with support for the P3 colour gamut and True Tone, you still get the blazing fast A12 Bionic chipset, and you also get the same 3GB of memory, Touch ID, stereo speakers, and cameras. Even more surprising is that the iPad mini also supports the 1st generation Apple Pencil, so you can still sketch, draw, and make super accurate taps.

You might think that the iPad mini display features less pixels that its larger siblings, but you'd be wrong because the iPad mini manages to cram 3-million pixels into its 7.9-inch display. With support for the P3 colour gamut, an antireflective coating, plus 500 nits of brightness, the iPad mini display manages to look colourful, bright, and crisp wherever you are; even when you're outdoors in the sunshine.

The iPad mini is just an amazing tablet that can be held comfortably in one hand, and it slips into a rucksack or purse without adding any considerable weight. It's a tablet which you can leave lying around the house, yet it doesn't take up any space.

Pros:

- Very comfortable to hold.
- Small and light makes it easier to carry.
- Affordable.

Cons:

- Only supports the first-generation Apple Pencil.
- No face recognition.
- No ultra-wide camera.
- Two speakers, rather than four.
- The small screen makes multitasking and productivity apps difficult to use.

iPad Air

The iPad Air pretty much is an iPad Pro; well the 10.5-inch 2017 iPad Pro. It looks almost the same, it's packed with some seriously fast hardware, it supports the same Smart Keyboard, and it also works with the Apple Pencil (albeit the first-generation Apple Pencil). Think of the iPad Air as the previous-generation iPad Pro, at a much-reduced price.

Let's talk about specifications for a moment, because packed within the iPad Air is Apple's most powerful mobile CPU: the A14 Bionic Chip. It's manufactured using a 5-nanometer process, which manages to cram 11.8 billion transistors which are split across six cores. As a result, the iPad offers a huge jump in performance while also managing to be faster than most PC laptops.

You might be wondering where the Touch ID fingerprint sensor is located on the iPad Air. It's actually neatly tucked away *inside* the power button, on the top of the device. It's the smallest Touch ID sensor Apple has ever produced, and because it's integrated into the power button, you can turn on and unlock your iPad Air with just one press of your finger.

So who is the iPad Air aimed at? It's not aimed at professionals, because they're far more likely to be tempted by the latest iPad Pro; and it's not aimed at those who want a tiny tablet to carry around, because the iPad mini covers that segment. Instead, the iPad Air is aimed at those who just want a *really good iPad*. An iPad which covers all of the classic iPad stuff (like gaming, watching movies, and browsing the web), but which also supports an excellent typing experience thanks to support for the Smart Keyboard.

Pros:

- Similar specs to the iPad Pro, but considerably cheaper.
- Large 10.5-inch display.
- Thinner and lighter than the regular iPad.
- Touch ID is convenient for those wearing a face mask.

Cons:

- Only supports the first-generation Apple Pencil.
- No ultra-wide camera.
- Two speakers, rather than four.

iPad Pro

An entirely new camera system, faster internals, and double the storage, make the latest iPad Pro a powerful alternative to traditional desktop computing.

Glance at either the 11-inch or 12.9-inch iPad, and you might struggle to tell them apart from the earlier models. That's because from the front and the sides, they look identical in every way. It's not until you look around the back that you'll notice a pretty big difference: a dual camera system with a LIDAR scanner for depth sensing and Augmented Reality (AR).

This all-new camera system is a massive upgrade over previous iPad Pros. Both the 12MP camera, and the 10MP ultra-wide camera, are borrowed from the iPhone 11. They take amazing photos - even in low light conditions. The LIDAR scanner is the first of its kind on any type of computing device. With support from third-party apps, it should enable faster and more accurace AR experiences, such as games which blend with the real world around you. With time, it might also enable you to take more accurate Portrait Mode photos.

Pros:

- Massive 12.9-inch display makes drawing and working with productivity apps easy.
- Beautiful display that reaches to the edge of the device.
- Can replace a laptop computer.
- Supports latest Apple Pencil, plus the Magic Keyboard.
- AR sensor on the back future-proofs the iPad Pro.

Cons:

- 12.9-inch iPad is heavy, especially with the Magic Keyboard case.
- Expensive.

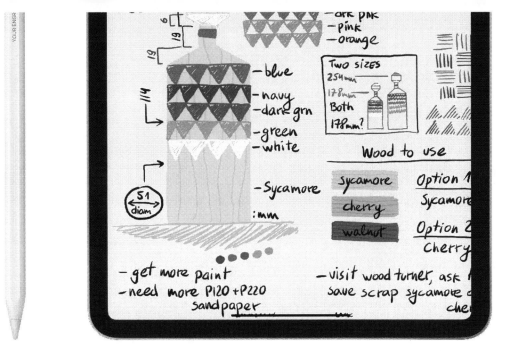

Liquid Retina Display

The Liquid Retina display which dominates the front of iPad Pro is a beautiful thing to behold. Perhaps that's because of the sheer size of the display, which makes it possible to create content or enjoy media in a way that isn't possible on the iPhone.

The Liquid Retina display on the iPad Pro 11-inch has a resolution of 2388x1668 at 264 pixels per inch, and a pixel density of 264 pixels per inch. The 12.9-inch model has a resolution of 2732x2048, also at 264 pixels per inch. That's the same density as the previous iPad Pros, so if you've upgraded from any of those devices, then you'll be familiar with how sharp it looks.

Both displays support the P3 wide colour range, which enables richer reds and more vibrant greens, but at 600 nits maximum brightness support, they're not quite bright enough to support the full HDR format. Apple defines the displays on the iPad Pros as "EDR" compatible, which stands for extended dynamic range. This means you can still download and watch HDR-supported content, such as the latest shows from Netflix, and they will look nearly HDR in colour and brightness quality; but the only way to truly watch them in HDR is to use a USB-C cable, then mirror your iPad's display on a HDR-supported screen.

An anti-reflective coating has been applied to the iPad Pro display, to help hide reflections and glare across the screen, and it's better than any previous iPad, or any of Apple's other portable devices. It can also hold up over time to heavy-duty Apple Pencil use, alongside the tens of thousands of prods and pokes that come with being a multi-touch display.

One obvious difference between the latest iPhones and the iPad Pro is a lack of a notch. Because of its relative size, the bezels around the iPad Pro are large enough to house some of the most sophisticated technology ever developed for an iPad. Called the TrueDepth Camera System, it contains the following sensors and emitters to enable face recognition:

- Ambient light sensor
- Speaker
- Proximity Sensor
- Flood Illuminator

- Microphone
- 7MP camera
- Infrared Camera
- Dot Projector

The TrueDepth Camera System enables you to unlock your iPad using just your face. Introduced alongside the iPhone X in 2017, it has proved to be a more efficient system than the fingerprint sensor included with previous iPhones and iPads.

On the iPad Pro, the TrueDepth sensors are located at the "top" of the device in portrait mode, but unlike with the iPhone, you can use FaceID to unlock your device in whichever orientation the iPad is in. To do this, the team at Apple captured hundreds of thousands of facial geometry samples, to create a more complex model for more complex training; which basically means the iPad Pro learns how to recognise your face over time.

Placing the TrueDepth camera on the top of the iPad Pro poses one small problem: if you're holding the iPad in landscape orientation, then the TrueDepth sensor can become blocked by your hand. The iPad will notify you if this happens, with a message on-screen that reads "Camera covered". It will also show an animated arrow pointing to where the camera is. With time, it becomes a natural habit to hold the iPad Pro in a way that doesn't cover the camera.

Industrial Design

The iPad Pro features a design language that in many ways, is a throwback to the iPhone 4 from a decade earlier. Gone are the rounded edges and chamfered detailing found on the traditional iPad; instead, replaced with flat edges that fall off, and stark antenna lines that are hard to miss. It's industrial to behold, and surprisingly attractive in person. It moves the design language forward, while staying true to its heritage.

Some design choices from earlier iPad models remain, however. The power button is still at the top of the device, unlike on the side, as seen with the latest iPhone models, and the volume buttons remain on the upper-right side.

Beneath the volume buttons, centred along the side of the iPad, is a magnetic connector for the Apple Pencil. Look around the back and you'll see the Smart Connector near the bottom of the iPad, which lets you wirelessly connect the new Magic Keyboard. Thanks to its clever design, the Smart Connector is both dust and waterproof, while also providing power to the keyboard.

By now you might have noticed that the traditional 3.5mm headphone socket no longer exists. Apple has been dropping support for 3.5mm headphones from its products for quite some time, which has helped them to introduce the bezel-to-bezel curved display (a 3.5mm socket goes deep into the device and prevents the LCD from reaching the edges). If you've already gone wireless with your headphones, then these will work perfectly with the iPad Pro; otherwise, you'll need to purchase a USB-C to 3.5mm Headphone Jack Adaptor from the Apple Store.

A12Z Bionic

The iPad Pro has always been a competitor to notebooks when it comes to raw speed. The latest iPad Pro takes things further. It's faster than most laptops on the market today, and even faster than the 13-inch MacBook Pro, no matter which processor the notebook is configured with.

In short, the A12Z chip inside the iPad Pro is a *beast*. Its 7-nanometer design is based on the A12X Bionic from the previous iPad Pro; and it still retains a similar 8-core design. When compared to previous iPads, Apple says the A12Z chip is up to 35 percent faster on single-core performance, and up to 90 percent faster on multi-core processes.

The GPU (graphics processing unit) within the iPad Pro also features a 7-core design, which Apple says is comparable to an Xbox One in terms of graphics rendering. We're unlikely to see any games which can prove that in the near future, but for now, it's great for high-end professionals who demand the fastest GPUs for rendering imagery.

Tech Specs

Internals:
- 11-inch screen: 2388x1668 LED
- 12.9-inch screen: 2732x2048 LED
- Processor: A12Z Bionic chip
- RAM: 6GB
- Speakers: 4-speaker audio
- Camera: 12MP wide lens, 10MP ultra-wide lens, LIDAR scanner, and 7MP front-facing lens
- 11-inch Battery: 29.37-watt-hour
- 12.9-inch Battery: 36.71-watt-hour
- Storage: 128GB / 256GB / 512GB / 1TB

11-inch iPad Pro Dimensions:
- Height: 9.74"
- Width: 7.02"
- Thickness: 5.9mm
- Weight: 468 grams

12.9-inch iPad Pro Dimensions:
- Height: 11.04"
- Width: 8.46"
- Thickness: 5.9mm
- Weight: 631 grams

Cameras

Hold an iPad Pro in your hand, and the first thing you might *feel* is the camera bump around the back.

That's because the iPad Pro is thinner than the camera module mounted within, meaning the lenses now poke out of the back. On the downside, it means the iPad wobbles slightly when laid flat, but on the upside, the latest iPad Pro includes the same amazing lenses found on the iPhone 11.

The top camera is a new 12MP wide camera with a new sensor that has a faster autofocus. In low-light conditions, it's now up to 3X faster than the previous generation of the iPad. The lower lens is a brand new ultra-wide camera with a 120-degree field of view, enabling you to capture more in your photos, like a stunning landscape or a group shot. Think of it as an optical 2X zoom out, so you can capture more without moving.

The front-facing camera now supports limited 3D depth, to enable Portrait selfies and Memojis. This means you can now take selfie photos with a blurred background, to simulate traditional DSLR cameras, or bring your face to life with animated characters including a dinosaur, alien, or unicorn.

Wide Camera

- 26 mm focal length
- f/1.8 aperture
- 6-element lens
- Optical image stabilization
- 100% Focus Pixels
- New 12MP sensor

Ultra Wide Camera

- 13 mm focal length
- f/2.4 aperture
- 5-element lens
- 120° field of view
- 4x more scene
- 10MP sensor

LIDAR

By now you've probably noticed the mysterious grey circle on the camera bump. It's a custom-designed LiDAR scanner that uses direct time of flight to measure reflected light from up to five metres away, both indoors and out. In short, it can instantly work out the dimensions of the environment around to you to enable accurate 3D augmented reality experiences. This means you can place a virtual object in the room in front of you, then see objects pass both behind and in front of it. With time you can expect to see more immersive and realistic games and AR apps.

Audio

More people than ever before are using their iPad to watch TV shows, movies, and stream video content, so it's essential that the audio speaker system is capable of producing rich, deep sound that carries across a room. The iPad Pro achieves this by using four high-fidelity speakers, with one in each corner. This layout produces an engaging sound with three times the acoustic output of the iPad Air, making video content and apps sound better than ever before. Additionally, the iPad Pro automatically adjusts the orientation of high-frequencies depending on how you're holding the device, ensuring that the top two speakers are always dedicated to higher frequencies.

Still wondering which iPad to get?

Some helpful tips for deciding whether to go Air, iPad, or mini...

If the last few pages didn't help, then here are some examples of how each model of iPad suits different lifestyles and choices...

"All I need is the basics"

If you just want to check emails, browse the web, and look at Facebook, then the regular iPad is the choice for you. Now all you need to do is pick a colour. You can choose from silver, space grey, or gold.

"I want the smallest iPad"

The iPad mini is the perfect portable tablet. With its 7.9-inch display, it's small enough to be held in one hand, yet it still supports every iPad app, and the Apple Pencil.

"I'm pretty creative and/or productive"

If you're planning on sketching, painting, working with 3D models, or doing anything else creative, then the iPad Pro is your best choice. It has the largest screen of all the iPads, coming in at either 11 or 12.9-inches, which makes creating things much easier.

"I want to play games and watch a lot of movies"

With its large 12.9-inch display, the iPad Pro is the best choice for both gaming and media consumption. The bigger screen makes watching high-definition video content more immersive, while also making it easier to control games.

"I m on a budget, and just want an iPad"

If all you need is a new iPad, and you don't want to spend a fortune to get the latest specifications, then get the regular 9.7-inch iPad. It doesn't have a True Tone display, and the camera isn't the best, but it covers all the basics, and still makes for a fantastic tablet.

The iPad buttons

A quick overview of what each physical button does...

Unbox your iPad for the first time and you'll likely marvel at its machine-polished aluminium body and large glass screen. Then you'll notice the physical buttons which run along the edges. Here's what each of those buttons do when you press and hold them...

iPad Pro and iPad Air:

Power Button

When off:

- Press and hold to turn your iPad Pro on. On an iPad Air, this also acts as a fingerprint sensor.

When on:

- Press it once to lock your iPad.
- Press and hold along with a volume button to turn off your iPad.
- Press and hold to enable Siri.
- Press it twice to access Apple Pay.

Volume Up

- Press once to turn the volume up.
- Press and hold to quickly turn the volume up.
- Press while using the Camera app to take a photo.
- Press simultaneously with the Power button to take a screenshot.

Volume Down

- Press once to turn the volume down.
- Press and hold to quickly mute the audio.
- Press while using the Camera app to take a photo.

iPad and iPad mini:

Power Button

When off:
- Press and hold to turn your iPad on.

When on:
- Press it once to lock your iPad.
- Press and hold to turn off your iPad.

Volume Up

- Press once to turn the volume up.
- Press and hold to quickly turn the volume up.
- Press while using the Camera app to take a photo.
- Press simultaneously with the Home button to take a screenshot.

Volume Down

- Press once to turn the volume down.
- Press and hold to quickly mute the audio.
- Press while using the Camera app to take a photo.

Home Button

- Return to the Home screen.
- Press and hold to enable Siri.
- Press it twice while locked to access Apple Pay.
- Press it twice while unlocked to open the Multitasking screen.

Setup and activate your iPad

Discover how to activate your brand new iPad...

So you've bought a brand new iPad, and you've unwrapped it from the box. The next step is to activate it for the very first time. This process will let you choose a language to use, set your location and local time, and activate key features such as Siri (a helpful voice-activated assistant). Once your iPad is activated, you'll be able to use it to browse the web, send messages, plus much more.

How to insert a SIM card (iPad with cellular only)

1. Look in the iPad box for the SIM tray tool. It's thin, silver, and looks like a paperclip.

2. Insert the pointy end of the SIM tray tool into the small hole on the right-side of your iPad.

3. Press hard, and the sim tray will pop out slightly.

4. Use your fingernail to pull the sim tray out, then carefully place your SIM card into it. You might have to flip it around to make sure it fits property.

5. Slide the SIM tray back into your iPad and you're good to go.

Activate your iPad

1. Start by turning on your iPad for the first time. To do this, just press the **power** button on the upper-right side. After a moment or two the Apple logo will appear.

2. When the Hello screen appears, **swipe up** from the bottom of the screen to continue.

3. Tap the language you want to use for your iPad, then tap the country or region.

If you're moving from one iPad to another...

Use the Quick Start tool to copy across your old iPad

If you're going from an old iPad to a new one, then you can use the Quick Start tool to automatically copy across all of your messages, photos, apps, settings, and personal data to the new iPad. It works quickly and it's easy to do...

1 Place your new iPad next to your old one. The Quick Start screen will automatically offer the option of using your Apple ID to set up the new device. Make sure it's the right Apple ID, then tap **Continue**.

2 Wait for an animation to appear on your new iPad, then use the camera viewfinder on the old iPad and centre the animation in the middle of the screen. When you see a button that says **Finish on New [Device]**, tap the button and follow the on-screen options to transfer your apps, data, and settings to the new device.

Use the Quick Start tool to copy your data from iCloud

If you don't have your old iPad to hand, then you can sync all of your messages, apps, accounts, and other personal data from iCloud. To do this:

1 After activating your iPad, tap **Restore from iCloud Backup**.

2 Sign into iCloud using your Apple ID and password.

3 Choose the most recent backup. You can check by looking at the date and size of each backup.

4 If you've purchased apps and iTunes content using multiple Apple IDs, then you'll be asked for the passwords to each one.

5 Wait for the process to finish. This may take some time, so it's a good idea to keep your device connected to Wi-Fi and a power source.

6 After the process has completed your iPad will turn on and activate, but it will still need to download content such as apps and photos, so be patient as it restores all of your data.

The very basics

Discover the first steps to using your iPad...

Powering on and off

To turn on your iPad, press and hold the **Power** button until the screen turns on.

To turn your iPad off, hold the **Power** button on a regular iPad or iPad mini, or the **Power** button and the **volume down** buttons on the iPad Air and Pro, until the screen dims, then move the power slide towards the right.

Sleep mode

Your iPad will automatically lock itself and go into sleep mode if left alone for 2 minutes. When it's asleep it will still check for new messages, and let you know when a phone call comes through, but the screen will be turned off and it will use less power.

To put your iPad to sleep, tap the **Power** button once.

To wake your iPad up, either tap on the screen or press the **Power** button once.

Adjust sleep mode

To adjust the length of time it takes for your iPad to go into sleep mode, open the **Settings** app, tap on **Display & Brightness**, then tap **Auto-Lock**.

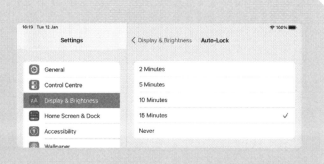

Access Control Centre

Think of Control Centre as a place where you can change the screen brightness, adjust the volume, and access several other settings. You can always find it by swiping your finger downwards from the very top right corner of the screen.

Adjust the volume

You can use the two buttons on the right side of your iPad to turn the volume up or down. You can also press and hold one of these buttons to quickly turn the volume to its maximum setting, or mute it. You can also adjust the volume from Control Centre. Just swipe the volume slider up or down. You can tap and hold on this slider to make it bigger too.

Change the brightness

You can adjust the screen brightness in two ways. The first is to open Control Centre, then use the brightness slider on the right side. Alternatively, open the **Settings** app, tap on **Display & Brightness**, then use the **Brightness** slider.

Lock the screen orientation

When you turn your iPad on its side, the screen will rotate itself to match the orientation. To prevent this from happening, position your iPad in the orientation you wish to keep, open Control Centre, then tap the button with a **padlock** in its centre.

Touch ID

Setup Touch ID so you can unlock your iPad using your fingerprint...

A fingerprint is one of the most secure methods of locking your iPad, because afterall, the chances of someone else with the same fingerprint coming across your iPad is pretty small. Using your fingerprint to unlock your iPad is also pretty efficient, because it takes less than a second for your iPad to read your print and unlock the device.

Keeping your personal data safe is one of Apple's most pressing priorities, so here's what the company does to ensure your fingerprint never leaves your iPad:

- The iPad and its operating system can never access your fingerprint data. Only the fingerprint sensor beneath the Home button can access your print, and it only sends a yes or no signal to the operating system when you place your fingertip on the sensor.

- Your fingerprint never leaves the physical device. That means it can't be accessed by the NSA, hackers or anyone else.

Set up Touch ID

Your iPad will ask you to setup Touch ID when you activate it for the very first time. If you skipped that step, just open the **Settings** app, select **Touch & Passcode** then tap **Add a Fingerprint.**

Place your thumb or finger on the **Home** button. You'll see a graphic of a fingerprint appear and start to turn red. Keep placing your fingerprint on the Home button until the graphic has completely filled.

You'll then be asked to repeat the process, but this time to place the edges of your finger on the Home button. Once you've finished, tap **Continue** to add your fingerprint.

Place Your Finger

Lift and rest your finger on the Home button repeatedly.

Give each fingerprint a name

If you're adding multiple fingerprints, then it's a good idea to give them names. This helps you to manage the prints of multiple people, or work out which ones to delete at a later time. To do this, go to **Settings** > **Touch & Passcode,** then tap on the fingerprint you wish to name.

How to delete a fingerprint

To remove a fingerprint, go to **Settings** > **Touch & Passcode,** then tap on the fingerprint you wish to delete. Next, tap the red **Delete Fingerprint** text.

Face ID

Unlock your iPad Pro or iPad Air using your face...

If you own an iPad Pro then you've likely notice it doesn't have a Home button or fingerprint sensor. Instead, a small array of sensors above the screen scan your face, then automatically unlock your iPad Pro in the blink of an eye. It's a feature called Face ID, and it's way more advanced than you might think.

It works by using a TrueDepth Camera System to recognise you. Basically, an infrared camera can see your face, even in the dark, while a dot projector maps your face with more than 30,000 dots. All of this data is used to create a mathematical model of your face. This mathematical model is used to prevent people from using photos of you to unlock your iPad. Face ID also looks for telltale signs of life (like moving or blinking eyes), to know that a model of your face wasn't used. Once it has confirmed all of this (which usually takes less than a second) then Face ID tells your iPad that it's definitely you; and that things are good to go.

Set up Face ID

Your iPad will ask you to setup Face ID when you activate it for the very first time. If you skipped that step, just open the **Settings** app, select **Face ID & Passcode** then tap **Enrol Face.**

Follow the on-screen instructions to add your face. You'll be asked to gently move your head in a circular motion. That's because Face ID performs best when all angles of your face are captured. Once the process is complete, tap **Done** to enrol your face.

Create an alternative look

If you sometimes change your look in a drastic way (for example via makeup, with a wig, or with extensive accessories), then you can teach Face ID to recognise you with these changes. To do this, get ready with your alternative look, then go to **Settings > Face ID & Passcode**, then tap **Set Up an Alternate Appearance**.

Lock your iPad with a passcode

Set a six-digit passcode to keep prying eyes out...

Your iPad contains incredibly personal information that only you should have access to, such as photos, messages, bank account details, and passwords. On the last two pages, we looked at enabling either Face ID or Touch ID to lock your iPad and keep it secure, but you can also enable a six-digit passcode lock. This acts as a failsafe for when Touch or Face ID isn't available (such as when you're wearing gloves or a face mask). You can use any set of numbers for your passcode lock, but make sure it's something memorable. Here's how it works:

Turn on passcode lock

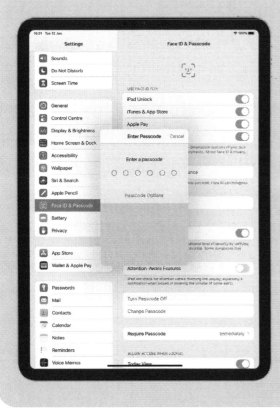

1 Open the **Settings** app. It's grey and has a cogwheel in its centre.

2 Scroll down, then tap **Face ID & Passcode**. If you have an iPad or iPad mini, then it will say **Touch ID & Passcode**.

3 You will see a number of options related to Face or Touch ID. To find the passcode lock option, scroll down, then tap **Turn Passcode On**.

4 You'll be asked to enter a six-digit passcode. Make sure it's something memorable that you only you know. Re-enter the code to confirm when asked.

5 If you're unhappy with your six-digit passcode, then you can always return to this settings panel and tap **Change Passcode** to create a new one.

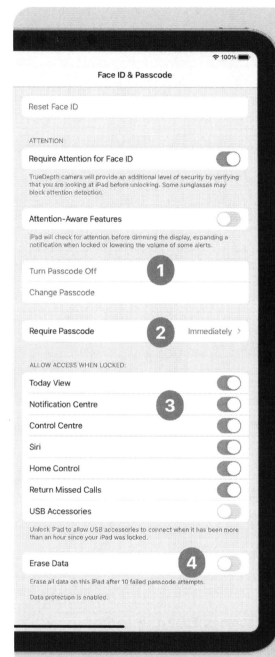

Passcode options

1 If you need to change your passcode at any time, tap this option and enter a new one.

2 Select this option to select how long you need to wait before entering your passcode again. If you have Face ID or Touch ID enabled, then this will always default to immediately.

3 When your iPad is locked, it's still possible to do a number of things even without entering a passcode. By toggling these options off, you can prevent someone from using Siri, replying to a message, and more.

4 You iPad can automatically erase itself if someone enters the wrong passcode more than 10 times. Toggle this option on to activate this feature.

Adjust the display

Learn how to adjust the display to meet your needs...

The display of your iPad is its most crucial component because it's the one you spend the most time prodding, poking, and looking at. You might not know it, but there are some essential settings available for the iPad which let you adjust the screen to suit your needs better. You can play around with the brightness, make text bigger, and capture what's on the screen to share with others...

Adjust the brightness

If you'd like to adjust the brightness of the display, just swipe down from the top-right corner of the screen to access Control Centre, then slide the **brightness** slider up or down. You can also **tap and hold** on the slider to enable a larger version that's easier to control.

Disable True Tone

True Tone is a clever feature that adjusts the colour tone of the display to match the environment around you. So if you're sitting in a room with yellowish light, the screen will subtly change to suit the environment.

If you prefer the screen to always look pure white, open the **Settings** app and go to **Display & Brightness,** then toggle **True Tone** off. You can also disable True Tone from Control Centre. Just tap and hold on the brightness slider, then tap the **True Tone** button.

Disable Auto-Brightness

By default your iPad will automatically adjust the brightness of the display to match the conditions of your environment; so if you're in a dark room, the screen will dim, while under direct sunlight it will set to maximum brightness.

To turn this off or on, go to **Settings** > **Accessibility** > **Display & Text Size** and turn **Auto-Brightness** off.

Adjust the Auto-Timer

If you'd like to adjust how long it takes until your iPad locks itself and turns off the display, go to **Settings** > **Display & Brightness** > **Auto-Lock**. From there you'll find several settings that range from 1 minute to never.

Toggle Dark Mode

With Dark Mode you can give all the default apps an evocative new look, where whites become black, folder backgrounds and the Dock take on a smokey look, and the default wallpapers supplied by Apple take on a darker look. There are two ways you can turn on (or off) Dark Mode:

1 Access Control Centre, tap and hold on the **brightness** slider, then tap the **Dark Mode** button in the bottom-left corner.

2 Open the **Settings** app, select **Display & Brightness**, then tap the **Dark** option at the top of the screen.

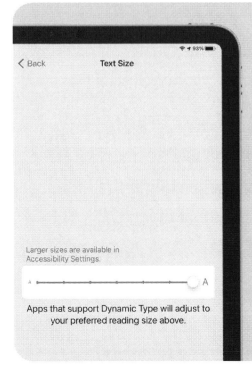

Make text bigger

If you're finding it difficult to see text on the iPad's screen, then it's possible to increase text size for everything you see and tap on. To do this:

1 Open the **Settings** app, then choose **Display & Brightness.**

2 Scroll down to the bottom of this panel, then tap **Text Size**.

3 Use the slider to adjust text size. Move the slider to the right and everything will get bigger. Move it left and everything will get smaller.

4 To return to the regular text size, return to this panel then move the slider to the centre position.

The basics of using apps

Learn what an app is, how to open and close apps, plus more...

Take a look at your iPad's screen and you'll see a number of small icons going from top to bottom. Each of these icons represents an individual app on your iPad. Look closely, and you'll see an app for taking photos, an app for accessing your calendar, an app for looking at Maps... the list goes on and on.

On this spread of pages we'll explore how to open and close apps, delete them, and organise them into folders.

Open an app

You can open any app on your iPad by lightly tapping on its icon. Just a quick tap of your fingertip is all that's needed.

Close an app

When you're ready to close an app and return to the home screen, just press the **Home** button on a regular iPad, or swipe upwards from the bottom of the screen on an iPad Pro or iPad Air.

Force an app to close

If you're using an app and it stops working, swipe upwards from the bottom of the screen then stop after a few inches. You'll see a grid of recently opened apps appear. To force quit the app you were just using, slide it upwards off the top of the screen.

Delete an app

If you've downloaded an app but want to remove it, simply tap and hold on the app icon, wait a moment, then tap the **cross (x)** button that appears when the app starts to wiggle.

Tap and hold for options

You can **tap and hold** on most things on your iPad to access additional options, so tap and hold on an app and you can rearrange it or quickly jump to something within the app.

Create a folder of apps

It's a good idea to group similar apps into folders. For example, you might want to move all of your social media apps into a folder called "Social". To do this, **tap and hold** on an app, wait until it starts to wiggle, then drag it on top of another app. This will create a folder of apps. You can rename a folder by tapping and holding on its name.

Rearrange your apps

To move an app to another part of the screen, simply **tap and hold** on it until it starts to wiggle, then slide it somewhere else. You'll notice all the other apps rearrange and move out of the way as you go. When you've found a new location, tap **Done** in the top corner.

Manage Notifications

Discover how to manage notifications...

However you use your iPad, you're going to receive notifications on a regular basis. Notifications usually appear when you have a new message, or if an app wants to get your attention. If your iPad is locked, then the notification will appear as a bubble on the Lock Screen. If you're using your device when the notification arrives, then it will appear as a floating panel at the top of the screen. If an app wants to get your attention, then you might see a red dot above its icon on the Home screen.

If there's one annoying aspect about receiving notifications on an iPad, it's that you can't simply ignore them. Try to do that, and they'll only end up in the Notification Centre, forever awaiting an action from yourself. Similarly, if you try and ignore that little red dot above an app icon, and it'll never go away. Thankfully, you can customise, hide, and even disable notifications from individual apps...

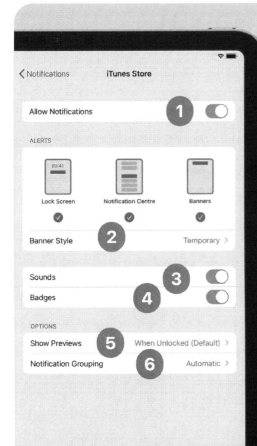

Customise notifications

To customise how apps notifiy you, go to **Settings > Notifications**, then select an app. On the following panel you'll see these options:

1 **Allow Notifications:** Toggle on to receive notifications from the app you selected.

2 **Banners:** Choose how you want notifications to appear when your iPad is unlocked. Tap **Temporary** to display alerts for a short period of time, or tap **Persistent** to have alerts stay on the screen until you act on it.

3 **Sounds:** Toggle audio alerts for when you receive a notification. Some apps, such as Messages, let you pick a custom sound too.

4 **Badges:** These appears as numbered red circles above an app icon. Uncheck this button to prevent badges from appearing over a specific app.

5 **Show Previews:** Choose what you want to see when you get a notification, like a text message.

6 **Notification Grouping.** Tap on this option to decide how multiple notifications from a single app appear on the Lock Screen.

Clear all your notifications

If you have a stack of notifications waiting for you in Notification Centre, then you can clear them all at once by tapping and holding on the small **X** button:

Interact with notifications

If a notification appears while you're using your iPad, pull it down from the top of the screen using your finger to interact with it. For example, if you get a message, pull the notification down and you'll be able to send a reply without going into the Messages app.

View grouped notifications

When you receive multiple notifications from the same source, then these will appear as a "stack" of notifications on the Lock Screen. By tapping on this stack, you can expand it. You can also swipe across a group of notifications to manage them, view them or clear them all away.

Manage notifications

If you receive an unwanted notification from an app or person, then you can customise how any further notifications from this source will appear. To do this, **swipe the notification to the left** then tap the **Manage** button. A small panel will then appear with two large buttons:

- **Deliver Quietly**
 Press **Deliver Quietly,** and any further notifications from this source will only appear inside Notification Centre, so you won't see any more Lock Screen notifications from this source, banners, app icon badges, or hear any sounds.

- **Turn Off**
 Press **Turn Off**, and you'll switch off all future notifications.

If you want to adjust notifications with more detail, then tap the **Settings** button at the bottom of the panel.

Connect to a Wi-Fi network

Easily connect to home, office, or public Wi-Fi networks...

Connecting to a Wi-Fi network is one of those fundamental tasks that we all must do from time to time. Perhaps you're visiting a friend and would like to hook up to their internet connection, or you might be sat in a coffee shop that offers free Wi-Fi. Here's how to do it:

1. Open the **Settings** app. It's grey and has a cogwheel in its centre.

2. Tap the **Wi-Fi** button. You'll see it near the top of the sidebar on the left.

3. If you live in a large house, then you should only see one Wi-Fi network. If you have neighbours nearby, then you might see multiple Wi-Fi networks available. That's because Wi-Fi signals can travel up to 50 meters, and even through walls. Think of it like a radio signal, and you'll get the idea.

4. Look for *your* Wi-Fi network then tap on it. If you don't which Wi-Fi network is yours, then you might need to ask whoever set it up for you. This might be a family member or friend, or it might be the network company.

5. After tapping on your Wi-Fi network, enter its password. If you don't know this, then try looking on the back of the Wi-Fi router. Usually a sticker can be found which contains the Wi-Fi password. You can also try asking whoever set up the Wi-Fi connection.

6. Tap the blue **Join** button on the keyboard. If you've entered the password successfully your iPad will automatically join the network.

What to do when the Wi-Fi stops working

If you're using the internet and it stops working, then you can usually remedy the problem by turning the router on and off again. To do this:

1 Look for the router. It's a small box connected to the phone line, and it likely looks like the image to the left. Often it has green blinking lights on one side. These lights indicate if the internet is working.

2 Restart the router. You can do this by pressing its power button, or by turning off the power at the wall, then back on again.

3 Wait for the router to turn back on. This can take up to two minutes, so be patient.

4 Hopefully, the internet will be working on your iPad again.

How to disconnect from a Wi-Fi signal

Sometimes you might need to disconnect from a Wi-Fi signal. Maybe you accidentally connected to it, or maybe you're in a hotel and don't want to pay for any further Wi-Fi access. To tell your iPad to forget about a Wi-Fi network:

1 Open the **Settings** app. It's grey and has a cogwheel in its centre.

2 Tap the **Wi-Fi** option in the sidebar.

3 Tap on the Wi-Fi network you wish to forget.

4 Tap Forget This Network.

Add an email account

Learn how to add your email account, calendar events, and passwords...

As you use your iPad to do day to day things, such as checking emails, adding calendar events, or logging into websites, then you're going to start accumulating login details, accounts, and passwords. On this page you'll learn the basics of adding an email account. Most of it happens automatically, and once you've added an account you'll be able to start emailing friends and family, check your calendar for events, plus much more.

Add your email account

1. Start by opening the **Settings** app, tap on **Mail**, then tap **Accounts**.

2. Tap on **Add Account**.

3. Select your email provider. If your email address ends with "gmail.com", then tap on Google. If it ends with "hotmail.com", select the Outlook option.

4. Your iPad will ask for the username and password associated with your email account. Simply enter these and tap **Next**.

5. Your device will verify your mail account details. Once the process has completed you can choose whether you wish to sync mail, contacts, calendar events, notes, and more using the toggle buttons.

Manually add an email account

If you have a custom email account – perhaps associated with work or a personal website - then it's possible to enter its details and access your emails through the Mail app. Adding an account isn't as easy as simply entering a username and password, you'll also need the server details and choose whether to use IMAP or POP3 (explained shortly).

1 Start by opening the **Settings** app, tap on **Mail**, then tap **Accounts**.

2 Tap on **Add Account**, choose **Other**, then tap **Add Mail Account**.

3 In the Name field, enter the name you wish recipients to see when they receive your email. Next, enter your email address and password used to access your account. In the Description field, enter a mail account name that's easily recognisable.

4 Tap **Next** and your device will attempt to verify the account. It will then ask you to choose an IMAP or POP account type. IMAP accounts store emails on a server, enabling you to check your email from multiple sources, i.e. your iPad and Mac. A POP account stores emails only on your iPad, meaning the account can only be accessed from that device.

5 Under Host Name, enter the server address for your email account. It might be something like imap. example.com. Next, enter your username once again in the User Name field, the outgoing server address and your password if required. Click **Next** and your device will verify the account.

6 If everything is correct, then you'll be ready to send and receive emails from your email account.

Calendar not syncing?

If you've added a Gmail or Outlook account, and don't see any events in the Calendar app, go to **Settings** > **Calendar** > **Accounts**, tap on your Gmail or Outlook account, then make sure the **Calendars** toggle button is on.

Connect to Bluetooth devices

Discover how to pair headphones and other Bluetooth devices...

The speakers in your iPad do a pretty good job at playing music and audio, but by connecting a set of Bluetooth headphones, you can enjoy audio at a volume level that won't interrupt anyone else. It's not just headphones that you can connect, because the iPad supports a massive number of Bluetooth devices, including gaming controllers, microphones, and even fitness equipment such as treadmills.

Connect a Bluetooth device

1. Open the **Settings** app, then tap **Bluetooth**.

2. Make sure the **Bluetooth** toggle switch is turned on.

3. Turn on the Bluetooth device you would like to connect to and make it discoverable. If you're not sure how to do that, read the device's instruction manual.

4. The Bluetooth device will appear in the OTHER DEVICES panel. Tap on it to connect. If the device is a computer or a vehicle, then you may need to enter a pairing code.

5. The device will connect and appear in the MY DEVICES panel. It is now ready to use.

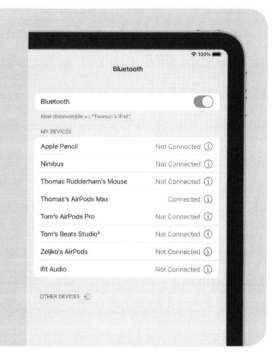

Connect a pair of AirPods

Think of AirPods as the next level in Bluetooth connectivity. When paired with your iPad, all you need to do is put them into your ears and they automatically connect, and when you take an AirPod out of your ear, the audio playback pauses.

Other thoughtful features included with the AirPod include:
- Support for Siri. Just tap on an AirPod twice then start talking.
- Connectivity with all your Apple devices. If you pause music on your iPad, then start playing music on your iPhone, the AirPods will automatically connect.
- Noise cancellation. Opt for the AirPod Pros, and you'll never be interrupted by background noise.

To connect a pair of AirPods to your iPad, simply open the case while your AirPods are near your iPad, and a setup animation will appear on the screen.

Bluetooth options

After a Bluetooth device has been paired, you can often customise it via the Bluetooth Settings panel. For example, if you connect a pair of AirPod Pros, then it's possible to toggle noise cancellation, press and hold options, perform an ear tip fit test, and even which ear acts as a microphone. To find these settings:

1. Open the **Settings** app, then tap **Bluetooth**.

2. Tap the **info (i)** button next to the device.

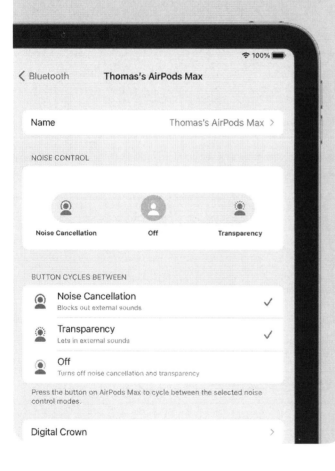

Swap between devices

If you're listening to music or talking to someone on the phone, and you want to swap from the speaker to your headphones, then:

1. Make sure the Bluetooth device is turned on and connected.

2. Swipe down from the top-right corner of the screen to access Control Centre.

3. Tap the **AirPlay** button. It's in the top-right corner of the music playback box.

4. Tap on the device you'd like to use.

4. While making a FaceTime or phone call, you can also tap the **Audio** button to swap between devices.

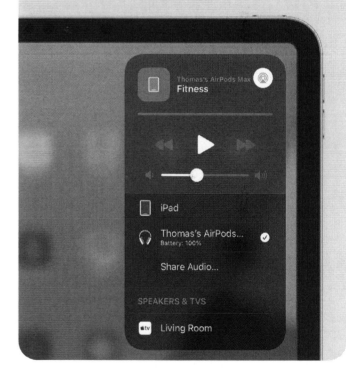

Disconnect from a device

If you no longer need to use a Bluetooth device, or you want to let someone else connect to it, then here's how to tell your iPad to disconnect from it:

1. Open the **Settings** app, then tap **Bluetooth**.

2. Tap the **info (i)** button next to the device, then tap **Forget This Device**.

The Lock Screen

Use gestures to unlock your iPad, access Notification Centre, and more...

Press either the **Home** or **Power** buttons on your iPad and the Lock screen will quickly fade into view. If you've received any notifications, such as a text message or a news story, then you'll see them in the middle of the screen. Otherwise, you'll just see the background wallpaper, time, and date.

1. Swipe down from the top-right corner to access Control Centre.

2. Tap a notification to find out more, or swipe it to the left to manage any further notifications.

3. Swipe from the left to access Spotlight, where all your widgets, shortcuts and Spotlight search can be found.

4. Swipe from the right to open the Camera app.

5. If using an iPad Pro, swipe up from the bottom of the screen to go to the Home Screen. If using an iPad, iPad mini, or iPad Air, press the **Home** button to go to the Home Screen.

The Home Screen

Discover how to interact with apps and folders...

From the Lock screen, swipe upwards from the bottom of the screen and your iPad will unlock and display the Home screen. You'll see multiple icons across the screen. These represent the apps installed on your iPad. To open one of these apps just tap on its icon. To close the app and go back to the Home screen, just swipe upwards from the bottom of the screen or press the **Home** button. You can also access the Dock at any time by swiping up from the bottom of the screen by just a small amount.

1
- Tap and hold on an app icon to see a secondary menu.
- Tap and hold on an app icon for three seconds to move, re-arrange, or delete apps.

2 To make a folder of apps, tap and hold on an app icon, wait for it to start jiggling, then drag the app on top of another.

3 Swipe left or right across an empty part of the screen to see more apps.

4 This is the Dock. You can put important apps here and you'll always find them at the bottom of the Home Screen.

Gestures and buttons

Learn about key gestures used for controlling your iPad...

The vast, high-definition screen that spreads out across your iPad is a technological marvel. You might not know it, but it actually supports up to 10 individual fingertips, and works by detecting the static charge on your skin — not heat or pressure as many often believe. By tapping and gesturing on the screen you can take full advantage of everything iOS has to offer, such as zooming into content, rotating images and more.

Additionally, the hardware buttons on your iPad enable you to activate Siri or shut the entire thing off. Many of these functions are entirely intuitive, but for those who have never interacted with an iPad before, let's go over them...

Return to the Home screen

Whenever you're in an app, swipe up quickly from the very bottom of the screen to return to the Home screen. On a regular iPad, iPad mini, or iPad Air, then you can also press the **Home** button.

Access the Dock

The Dock is where your favourite apps and most recently used apps are located. You'll see the Dock at the bottom of the Home screen, but you can also access it whenever you're in an app by swiping up from the bottom of the screen then stopping after an inch or two.

Access the multitasking screen

Swipe up from the bottom of the screen then stop halfway to see all the apps you've recently opened. If using a traditional iPad, then you can also press the Home button twice.

Force quit an app

While you're viewing the multitasking screen, push an app thumbnail upwards and off the screen to force quit it.

Power off your iPad

Hold down the **power** button. On the iPad Pro it's slightly more complicated: you need to hold down both the **power** button and **volume up** buttons.

Jump between apps

Swipe along the very bottom of the screen, left-to-right, and you'll jump between apps.

Access Search

From the Home screen, pull the screen down using your finger to access the Search screen. From here you can search for apps, emails, contacts and more.

Swipe to go back

To go back a panel or page, swipe from the left-side of the screen inwards. This works great in apps like Safari, Mail, or Settings.

Access Siri

To talk to Siri, press and hold the **Home** button. On the iPad Pro, press and hold the **power** button. You can also say "*Hey Siri*" out-loud to enable Siri.

How to use Control Centre

Discover how to quickly toggle controls...

Tucked above the screen are a helpful set of buttons for toggling settings and activating features. They include a slider for controlling the screen brightness, a button for enabling Wi-Fi, shortcuts to toggle Airplane Mode, Night Shift mode and more. To access these shortcuts at any time swipe down from the top-right corner of the screen.

You can long-press on any of these buttons to access further settings or controls that are easier to use. To close Control Centre, swipe back up or tap in the empty space below Control Centre.

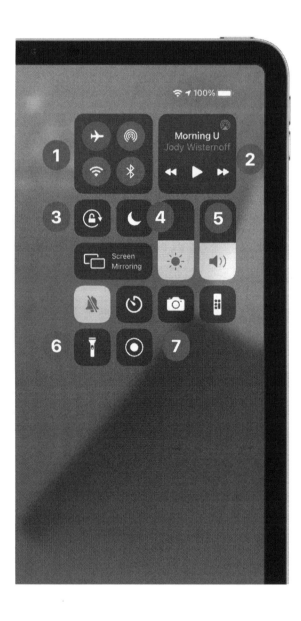

1 These four buttons enable you to toggle Airplane mode, your cellular connection, Wi-Fi, and Bluetooth. Tap and hold on this box to access controls for AirDrop and Personal Hotspot.

2 This box in the upper-right corner lets you control audio playback. If you have wireless headphones connected then you can connect to them using the AirPlay button in the very top corner of this box.

3 If you don't want the screen to rotate into landscape/portrait mode whenever you rotate your iPad, then tap the **Orientation Lock** button.

4 Tap the **moon** icon to turn on Do Not Disturb. While it's on you won't be bothered by FaceTime calls, texts or any notifications, and your iPad won't emit any noise and the screen won't turn on.

5 These sliders enable you to adjust the screen brightness and audio volume. You can tap and hold on each one to make it bigger and easier to use.

6 Tap the **Torch** icon to instantly turn on the flash at the back of your iPad Pro. You can also tap and hold to adjust the brightness.

7 Tap the **Timer** or **Camera** buttons to instantly open these apps.

Search your iPad

Search your iPad for apps and content

If you're looking for something specific on your iPad, such as a particular app or settings, then the search panel is often a good place to start. It can find nearly anything on your iPad, including content inside of apps. It can also search the web and make helpful suggestions.

There are two ways to access the search screen:

1 From the Home screen, swipe down from the middle of the screen and the search panel will appear. You can use this panel to look for messages, songs, notes, and even search for things on the web.

2 If you have a keyboard attached to your iPad, then hold the **Command** key and press the **spacebar** to access search. This works anywhere on your iPad, even when you're using an app.

Hide apps and app content from appearing in search results

You can adjust the search panel to hide individual apps and results while you're searching. To do this:

1 Go to **Settings** > **Siri & Search**.

2 Scroll down then select an app.

3 Untoggle **Show App in Search**, and **Suggest Content in Search** to prevent results and shortcut suggestions from appearing.

Type with the keyboard

The basics of the iPad's keyboard explained...

The software keyboard built into your iPad is amazing in several ways. It guesses what word you're trying to write, then automatically finishes it for you. It rotates with the screen to make typing easier. It can detect up to 10 fingertips to make typing quicker. You can hold down a key to see more options, plus much more. If you're new to typing on a glass screen then give it some time. The first few days might be frustrating as you work out how best to hold your iPad. Personally, I like to hold my iPad using both hands in the portrait orientation, and use my thumbs to type each key. However, for longer periods of typing, I prefer to rest my iPad horizontally on a surface, then type using both hands. Once you're comfortable typing, here are some tips for making the most out of the iPad's keyboard...

Make the keyboard bigger

To make the keyboard as big as possible, turn your iPad on its side. This will ensure the keys are as large as possible, making it easier for you to tap on each one.

How to use the shift key

Notice the two, upward-facing arrows on the left side of the keyboard. These are the shift keys. They let you type capital letters, or even write entire sentences in capital letters.

The upper shift key is broken into two parts. Tap on this once and you'll be able to type entire words and sentences in capital letters. When you've finished writing in capitals, tap it again and the keyboard will return to normal.

The lower shift key is a bit more flexible. Tap it once and only the next letter you type will be capital. Double-tap (quickly tap twice) it and all letters will be in capitals. You can also hold it down to type in capitals, then let go to return to lower case letters.

Enter numbers and symbols

Notice the button in either corner that says **.?123**. By tapping this you can access keys for entering numbers, symbols, and even currencies.

Dictate text, rather than type it

You can ask your iPad to listen to your voice and turn it into text. It works surprisingly well, and if done right can save a lot of time. Here's how it works:

Tap the button at the bottom of the keyboard that shows a microphone in it. You'll see the keyboard disappear, and a set of dotted lines appear instead. Your iPad is now listening to you. Speak out loud, and watch as your iPad enters text above the keyboard. If you need to enter a comma, simply say "comma". Similarly, if you need to enter a full stop, question mark, or exclamation mark, just say it out loud. When you've finished talking, press the small **keyboard** button at the bottom of the screen.

Send an emoji

Think of emoji as a second language. One made primarily of pictures, rather than words. You can use them to inject some humour into a sentence, such as in this example:

I absolutely 🤍 ☕ and 🍰

If you haven't already guessed, the above sentence says "I absolutely love coffee and cake".

To send an emoji, tap the smiley-faced button in the bottom corner of the keyboard. The emoji keyboard will them appear, containing smiley faces, animals, symbols, and even flags. You can swipe through them to explore each category, or tap one of the grey icons at the very bottom of the screen.

Tap the **A B C** button to close the emoji keyboard and return to the regular keyboard.

Type like a pro

Become a master at typing on the iPad keyboard...

Now that you're comfortable typing on the iPad's keyboard, it's time to take a look at some of its more intelligent and advanced features. You might not know from looking at it, but the iPad's keyboard is capable of guessing what you're trying to type. It can even let you enter symbols by flicking your finger upwards from a key. We'll explore all of these features, plus more on the following couple of pages.

Quickly select a word

By double-tapping two fingers on the keyboard you can quickly select a word. Double-tap then drag your finger and you'll be able to select multiple words or sentences.

Use predictive text

Predictive Text attempts to guess the next word you want to type and then offers it as a one-tap option above the keyboard.

To see predictive text in action, open the keyboard then start to type. As you enter each letter, a series of words will appear above the keyboard that guesses what you're trying to say. What makes predictive text really clever is that it learns who you're typing too and changes responses in relation to that person. So if you're talking to a close friend, predicted words will be relaxed and fun, but if it's your boss you'll see more formal and serious words appear.

Hide predictive text

If you'd like to hide or enable the predictive text panel just open the **Settings** app and go to **General > Keyboard** then toggle **Predictive** on or off.

Accents and extra keys

To add accents, extra letters and punctuation, **tap and hold** on a key. You'll see extra options and letters appear above your finger. To select one, simply drag your finger to it then let go.

Shortcuts

A shortcut is a quick and efficient way to send a common message. So type "omw" and your iPad will automatically write "On my way!" You'll find more shortcuts, plus the ability to create your own, by opening the **Settings** app, then tapping **Keyboard**.

Slide to type numbers

You can easily add a number by holding your finger on the **123** key, then sliding it to a number that appears.

Format text with the shortcut keys

As you use the iPad's keyboard for typing and entering text you'll probably notice the shortcut keys above they keyboard (if they don't appear then swipe the small grey bar above the keyboard upwards). Usually these enable you to cut, copy, paste, format text and attach images or files with just a tap of a button, but some apps may add further shortcuts.

Easily move the text cursor

If you'd like to quickly move the text cursor to another word or line, **press and hold** on the spacebar then use it as a trackpad with your finger.

Use Key Flick to quickly type symbols

Let's say you're typing a tweet and want to add the hashtag symbol. Using the iPad's Key Flick feature, you can simply press the **S** key then swipe down. You'll then see the key turn to an #, and the symbol appear wherever you're typing.

How to copy, paste, and select text

Discover how to copy something then paste it somewhere else...

Copying and pasting is a great way to move text or content from one app to another. For example, you could copy your address from Contacts and paste it into Safari, or copy a photo and then paste it into an email. The options are endless.

Copy and paste gestures

It takes some practice, but the best way to copy and paste text is to use a series of three-finger gestures. Start by selecting a piece of text (to do this just tap and hold on the text), then perform one of the following gestures:

- **Copy**: Perform a three-finger pinch.
- **Cut**: Three-finger double pinch.
- **Paste**: Three-finger pinch out.
- **Undo**: Swipe left with three fingers.
- **Redo**: Swipe right with three fingers.
- **Access a shortcut menu:** Three-finger tap.

When you successfully use one of the three-finger gestures you'll see a confirmation at the top of your screen.

Copy text

Find a source of text on your iPad, perhaps your phone number in Contacts. **Tap and hold** your finger on the number, let go when the magnifying glass appears, then choose **Copy** from the pop-up button.

Paste text

Next, close Contacts and open the Notes app. Create a new note by tapping the **plus** icon, then **tap and hold** on the empty note and choose **Paste**. Your phone number will appear in the new note.

Copy images

To copy an image from the Photos app, open it, tap the **Share** button in the top corner, then choose **Copy Photo**. You can now paste this image into a new email, SMS or iMessage.

Cursor navigation

You can pick up the cursor and drag it somewhere else.

Multiselect text

Quickly select a block of text by dragging your finger across it.

Intelligent text selection

You can select a word with a double tap, a sentence with three taps, and a whole paragraph with four taps.

Talk to Siri

Take command of your very own assistant...

Imagine Siri as your very own personal assistant. He (or she depending on your country of origin) can make FaceTime calls for you, dictate emails and messages, make a restaurant reservation, remind you to do things, tell you about movies, make jokes, and much more.

Siri isn't perfect, however. It can't remember interactions from the past, it relies on hearing your voice in a clear manner, and it needs a connection to the internet to work. If you're aware of these limitations and don't mind the odd false request, then Siri can save time and even be a little fun to use.

To enable Siri just hold down on the **Home** button on a regular iPad, or the **Power** button on the iPad Pro. After two seconds you'll hear Siri chime. You can now begin issuing commands, or if you're unsure, stay quiet and after a moment or two you'll see some of the things you can ask Siri.

Speak to Siri

Say out loud, "*What's the weather like today?*" Siri will automatically look for a weather report then tell you what it's going to be like. It's that simple to use Siri. When you're finished with Siri, press the **Home** button on a regular iPad, or the **Power** button on the iPad Pro, to return to where you were before.

Dictate text with Siri

If you'd like Siri to dictate a message or email, then simply say something like, "*Tell Noah I'll be late*". Siri will automatically create a new message or email to the recipient that says 'I'll be late home tonight'.

Activate Siri via voice command

It's possible to activate Siri by simply saying "*Hey Siri.*" After you hear the recognisable Siri chime, say a command out loud (such as "tell me the time") and Siri will respond – all without your touch. To enable this feature, go to **Settings > Siri & Search**, and turn on **Listen for "Hey Siri".**

Things you can ask Siri...

"Play something by Monsters and Men"

"Remind me to call Michael at 7."

"Send a message to Dave"

"Set up a meeting with Sarah at 9."

"Email Chris to say I'm running late."

"Show me movies directed by Steven Spielberg"

"How do I get to Tom's?"

"What is the Microsoft stock price?"

"Do I look fat in this?"

"What are your best chat-up lines?"

"What's 15 plus 26 plus 12 plus 4?"

"Roll the dice."
or
"Flip a coin."

"Schedule a haircut on Tuesday at 1 p.m."

Widgets

Add additional information to the Home Screen...

Think of widgets as small windows of helpful information that you can place around the Home screen of your iPad. You'll find widgets that display the latest news, widgets that display photos from your library, and even a "smart" widget, which changes throughout the day to show you helpful information.

There's one small caveat to widgets on the iPad: they only appear when you hold your iPad in landscape orientation. Nevertheless they're a helpful way to quickly access information from the Home Screen of your iPad.

Show widgets on the Home Screen

1 Open the **Settings** app, select **Home Screen & Dock**, look for the APP ICONS panel, then select **More**. This will make all of the app icons on the Home Screen slightly smaller, while also enabling you to stack widgets to the left-side of the screen.

2 Next, look below the APP ICONS panel, then toggle **Keep Today View on Home Screen** on.

3 Next, go back to the Home Screen, tap and hold on a blank space between apps and wait for the apps to start wiggling.

4 Tap the **plus (+)** button in the top-left corner of the screen to access the widget library.

5 A widget panel will then appear. You can scroll through it to explore the widgets available, or use the search bar at the top to quickly find a specific widget.

6 Tap on a widget and you'll see that it's available in various sizes. Select one, then tap **Add Widget** to add it to the Home Screen.

Rearrange widgets

If you're unhappy with the placement of widgets in the sidebar, then tap and hold on a widget until it starts to wiggle. Next, slide the widget around the screen using your finger. Once you've moved the widget to a suitable place, tap the **Done** button in the top-right corner.

Stack widgets

You can drag and drop one widget on top of another, and so long as they are both the same size, they will stack on top of each other. This means you can swipe vertically across the widget to go from one to another.

Edit widget stacks

Some widgets, such as "Smart Stack", let you reorder the content which appears within it. To do this, just tap and hold on the widget then choose **Edit Stack**. You'll then see a panel which lets you reorder or remove content.

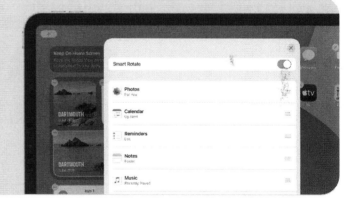

Delete widgets

To get rid of a widget, tap and hold on it until it starts to wiggle, then tap the **minus (-)** button.

Remove the widget sidebar

To remove the widget sidebar, tap and hold on an empty part of the Home Screen, wait for the app icons and widgets to start jiggling, then untick **Keep on Home Screen** in the top-left corner.

How to multitask

Use two apps at once, or watch a video while doing something else...

With the iPad, multitasking between two apps is a useful and realistic way to work. That's because of the sheer size of the iPad display, which makes it possible to run two full-sized apps at once, watch a video stream while browsing the web, or quickly check your emails while looking through photos. You can also access the Dock at any time, letting you quickly jump between your favourite apps.

There are three multitasking modes included with the iPad:

- Slide Over lets you quickly open a second app without leaving the one you're currently using.

- Split View enables you to run two apps at the same time.

- Picture in Picture lets you watch a video while still doing other things.

Let's take a look at all the multitasking features in a little more detail...

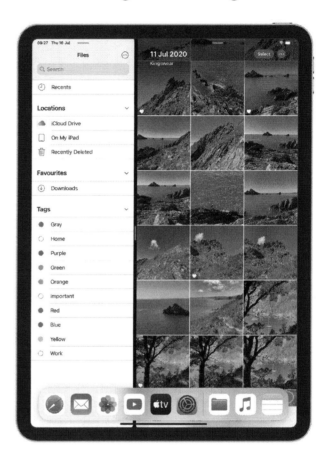

Explore the Dock

The Dock contains all of your favourite apps. You can always find it at the bottom of the Home screen. You can also access it when you're using an app by swiping up from the bottom of the screen then stopping after an inch or two. To close the Dock swipe it back down or tap in the space above it.

The Dock is split into two parts. On the left side are your favourite apps. You can add up to 8 apps at a time. To do this just visit the Home screen, tap and hold on an app then drag it onto the Dock. On the right side of the Dock are your three most recently opened apps.

Use Slide Over to control music

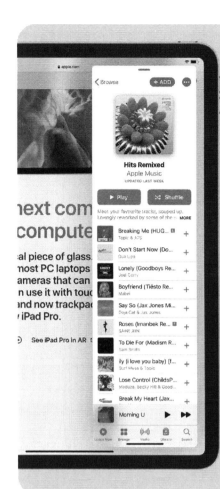

With Split View on iPad, you can call up a small, windowed view of an app (such as the Music app), and control both apps simultaneously:

1 Open the first app then slide your finger upwards from the bottom of the screen to access the Dock.

2 Drag the second app you wish to use from the Dock, and slide it towards the left or right side of the screen.

3 Let go of your finger and the app will hover in place. Slide View is now enabled.

To move a Slide Over app around the screen, place your finger on the top middle part of the app (where you see a grey line), then slide the app to its new position.

To snap a Slide Over app into place, so it can be run in Split View, tap the grey line then slide it upwards.

To dismiss a Slide Over app, simply slide it off the screen to the left or right. The app will still be there, even when you can't see it. You can bring it back by sliding your finger inwards from the side of the screen.

Run two apps at the same time

With Split View you can run two apps at the same time:

1 Open the first app then slide your finger upwards from the bottom of the screen to access the Dock.

2 Drag the second app from the Dock and move it to the far left or right of the screen. You'll see the app "snap" to the side of the screen. Let go and it will now appear as a Split View app.

You can resize apps by dragging the black bar from left to right.

To replace one app with another, open the Dock by swiping up the screen, then drag an app from the Dock and slide it over the app you wish to replace.

To close Split View, drag the black bar that separates the two apps off the screen.

Watch a video while doing something else

While watching a video in the TV app, tap the picture-in-picture button in one of the corners of the video window, and it will scale down to a corner of the display. You can now open a second app, check an email, or write an email while still watching your favourite TV show.

You can resize the video by pinching on it, or hide the video and continue listening to the audio by swiping the video to the side of the screen.

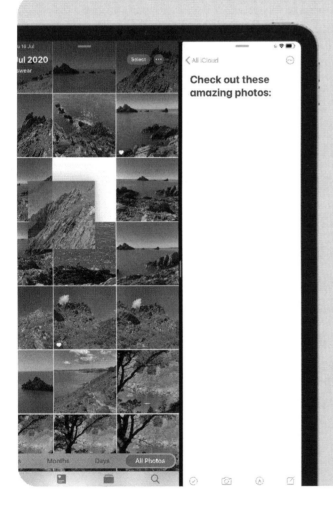

Use drag and drop to move things between apps

Drag and drop is a truly powerful tool on iPad, and it's simple to use. It works by letting you drag anything from one app to another. It can be an image, a link, a chunk of text... whatever you like. You can even drag multiple items at once to save time. It takes a little practice, but once perfected you'll wonder how you ever lived without this clever feature.

1. Let's start by running the Photos app and Notes app in either Split view. In the Photos app, tap and hold on a photo. After a moment it will lift off the screen and attach to your finger.

2. Next, slide the photo over to the Notes app. You'll see a small green icon appear when drag and drop is available. Once you see this let go. The photo will now be dropped into place. It's that simple!

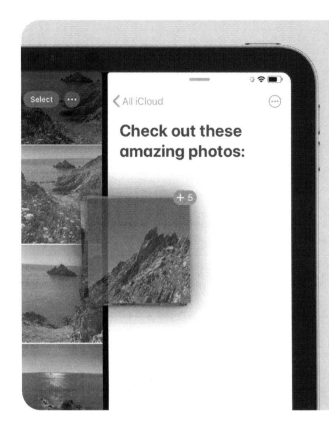

Check out these amazing photos:

How to drag and drop multiple items

While we're still looking at the Photos and Notes app...

1 **Tap and hold** on a photo, then wait for it to attach to your finger.

2 Tap on another photo and it will also attach to your finger (you might need to use two fingers to do this).

3 You can select as many photos as you wish using this technique.

4 Slide the photos over the Notes app and let go. They will all drop into place!

Drag and drop files into other apps

It's possible to drag items into another app that's not in Split or Slideover view. In fact, there are multiple ways you can drag items to another app. Begin by selecting an item (or multiple items), then:

- While tapping and holding on an item, return to the home screen with your other hand, open the app you wish to move the items to, then drop them into place.

- Use your other hand to swipe up from the bottom of the screen to enable the Dock, select the app then drop the item/s in place.

- Use four fingers and swipe across the screen to go between earlier apps. When you get to the right app, drop the item/s in place.

Passwords

Look up or manage your saved passwords...

Whenever you log into a website and enter a username, email address, or password, your iPad will ask if you would like to save these details on the device. If you agree, the next time you go back to the website and try to log in, your iPad will offer to automatically enter those details. It's a great time-saving feature, and it also means you don't have to remember every single password you've ever entered.

Sometimes you might need to take a look at these passwords and login details. Perhaps you're using someone else's computer and can't remember your password, or maybe you've accidentally saved multiple login details for a site and want to tidy them up. Here's how you can access every password and account saved on your iPad in a few steps...

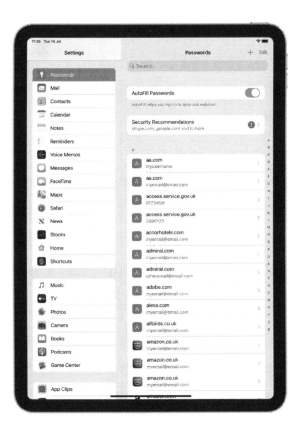

1. Open the **Settings** app, then tap on **Passwords**.

2. Your iPad will automatically scan your face (or ask for your fingerprint), to make sure it's you that's accessing your personal details.

3. You'll then see a list of every website you've ever logged into.

4. You can search for a website, username, email address, or password, by using the search field at the top of the screen.

5. You can add a new set of details by tapping the **plus (+)** button in the top-right corner.

6. To delete a set of details, swipe across the account from right to left, then tap the red **Delete** button.

Security Recommendations

Your iPad will automatically look for duplicate passwords, passwords that are easy to guess, or passwords that have leaked onto the web. If it finds any then it will list these at the top of the Passwords panel. Look for **Security Recommendations** below the search bar to find it. If any are available, tap on them, then tap **Change Password on Website** to update your details.

Reset your password using your iPad

If you have forgotten the password for your iPad (also known as your Apple ID), don't worry, as there are a couple of things you can try. The first is to change your password using your iPad. To do this:

1 Open the **Settings** app. It's grey and has a cogwheel in its centre.

2 Tap **[your name]** at the top of the screen, tap **Password & Security**, then tap **Change Password**.

3 If you are signed in to iCloud and have a passcode enabled, then you will be asked to enter the passcode for your device.

4 Follow the onscreen steps to update your password.

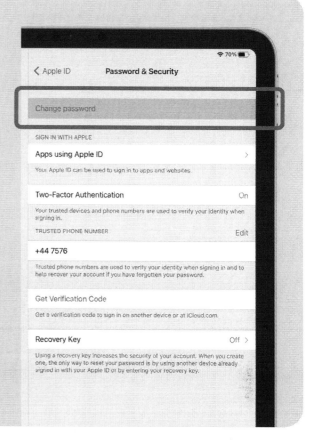

Reset your password on the internet

If the above steps didn't work, then you can try resetting your Apple ID password on the Apple website. To do this:

1 Use a web browser (such as Safari) and go to **iforgot.apple.com**

2 Enter your Apple ID. This is usually the email address you use to sign in.

3 Tap **Continue**.

4 If you have two-step verification enabled, then center your phone number, and follow the instructions to reset your password.

5 If you don't have two-step verification enabled, then follow the instructions to reset your password. You may have to enter security questions, or tap a link in an email.

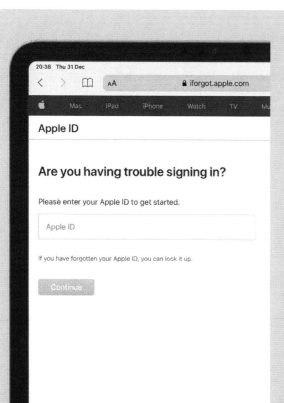

Share photos and files

Learn how to share something with other people or perform actions...

There's a lot you can do with a photo on your iPad. You can edit it (which we cover in the Photos chapter), share it with friends, hide it, duplicate it, print it, or even save it to the Files app. The same goes for other things on your iPad, like notes, reminders, and web pages. You can share all of these things (and more) by using the Share sheet, which you can access by pressing the Share button. It's usually tucked away in a corner, and it looks like this:

Share something with a friend

When you tap the Share button, you'll see contact suggestions near the top of the panel. These are based on your recent activity with friends and family, so you might see a shortcut to email something, attach it to a message or AirDrop it from one Apple device to another.

App shortcuts

Below the contact suggestions panel are a series of app shortcuts. If you decide to share a photo, you might see shortcuts for sending it within a message, posting it on Facebook, or attaching it within a note.

Other shortcuts

Scroll down the Share sheet, and you'll find a wide range of context-sensitive shortcuts. These are based on the thing you're sharing, so if it's a photo, you'll see shortcuts to hide it, duplicate it, or even make a watch face for your Apple Watch. Decide to share a web page, and you'll see shortcuts for adding a bookmark, finding a piece of on-page text and copying the URL.

Use AirDrop to share files

Send photos or files to friends nearby...

Have you ever wanted to share a photo, note, or video with someone else in the same room? So long as they also have an iPhone, iPad, or Mac, then it's possible to wirelessly transfer something with just a few taps. It works using a combination of Wi-Fi and Bluetooth, and there's no setup required. As a result it's never been quicker or easier to share files with friends, family and colleagues.

Enable AirDrop

To turn on AirDrop go to **Settings** > **General** > **AirDrop**. You can also use Control Centre. To do this open Control Centre, tap and hold on the box in the top-left corner, then tap **AirDrop**. On the following panel you can toggle AirDrop on or off, and choose who to share files with.

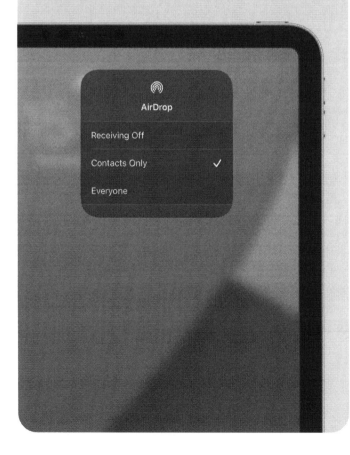

Share a file

Tap the **Share** button while viewing something you'd like to share. It's usually at the bottom of the screen. You'll see the AirDrop button near the middle of the Share sheet. Tap this and you'll see anyone nearby with AirDrop enabled. To share the file with them, just tap on their face or name.

Show your iPad's screen on the TV

Send video and music to your Apple TV...

If you're lucky enough to have an Apple TV, then it's possible to share movies, TV shows, music, and photos on your iPad straight to the television. This means you can start watching a movie on your iPad, then continue it on the TV. You can even mirror the entire iPad screen on the Apple TV, so other people can see what you're doing.

What is an Apple TV?

It's a small black box that plugs into your TV, one that's focused around entertainment, such as TV shows, movies, and music. It even has it's own app store, so you can download services such as Netflix, or even games.

What you can stream to an Apple TV:

- Movies, videos, and music
- Photos and slideshows
- Third-party video-based apps (such as Netflix)
- Your entire iPad display

Use your iPad as a TV remote

To do this, make sure your iPad and Apple TV are connected to the same Wi-Fi, swipe down from the top-right corner of the screen to access Control Centre, then tap the button which looks like a **TV remote**. You can then swipe across the large grey pad to move around the TV, adjust the volume, control playback, and even type with your iPad's keyboard.

Stream video or music to your Apple TV

1 Connect your iPad to the same Wi-Fi connection as the Apple TV.

2 Swipe down from the top-right corner of the screen to access Control Centre.

3 You will see a wireless icon in the top-right corner of the playback control window. Tap it to choose the Apple TV or AirPlay device.

4 If you've never connected your device to the Apple TV before, enter the 4-character passcode that appears on the TV.

To turn off AirPlay, return to Control Centre, tap the playback controls window, tap **AirPlay** then select your device. You can also press the **Back** button on the Apple TV remote.

Mirror your iPad display

Want to share your iPad screen on your Apple TV? It's easy, just swipe down from the top-right corner of the screen to access Control Centre, tap **Screen Mirroring** then choose the Apple TV.

Your iPad will immediately begin mirroring its display. While your screen is being mirrored everything you do on the iPad will appear on-screen, including messages, websites and apps. Note how the images rotates into landscape mode when your turn your device on its side. Also note, that if you view a photo or video while mirroring it will appear full-screen on the TV. To turn off mirroring, just bring Control Centre back up, tap the white **Apple TV** button, then tap **Stop Mirroring**. Alternatively, lock your iPad via the **power** button and the stream will end, or if you have the Apple TV remote to hand press the **Back** button.

Apple Pencil

There might be times when your fingertip isn't accurate enough for a creative process. Perhaps you'd like to draw a beautiful illustration, but your fingertip is getting in the way; or maybe you'd like to accurately select and manipulate an object that's mere pixels in size. With Apple Pencil, you can do all of that, and more.

That's because the Apple Pencil is sensitive to both tilt and pressure, enabling you to create a range of artistic strokes and effects. You can press harder to create a thicker line, or tilt the Apple Pencil to create subtle curves and shading. Apple Pencil also feels natural to hold, and there's practically no lag between the movement of the Pencil tip and the on-screen response. Using Apple Pencil with the iPad feels intimate, natural and intuitive. There are no buttons to learn, nor gestures to remember, just pick up Apple Pencil and start to draw.

How the Apple Pencil works

Thanks to some incredibly intricate and accurate pressure sensors — as well as two tilt sensors – the Pencil can calculate the exact orientation and angle of your hand. Your iPad recognises when Apple Pencil is being used, so to prevent spurious inputs it turns off Multi-Touch recognition to stop your palm and fingers from sending signals to the display. All this technology means you can quickly draw and sketch lines without the iPad missing a curve or swivel.

Tap sensitive

Whenever you want to change tools within an app, just double-tap the Apple Pencil. Using the Notes app, you can swap from the pen to the eraser with just two taps, and with third-party apps, you can configure the double-tap feature to suit your needs.

If you want to quickly get into the Notes app on your iPad, then tap the screen with the tip of the Apple Pencil and you'll automatically unlock the device and jump straight into the Notes app.

It's magnetic

The first generation of Apple Pencil was a bit fiddly to charge. First, you had to pull off its cap, then plug the top of the Pencil into the Lightning Port on the bottom of the iPad. The second generation of Apple Pencil supports wireless charging; so to charge it, just snap the Pencil to the side of your iPad.

The magnet is stronger than you might think too, so you can carry your iPad, or even shake it, and the Pencil won't drop off.

First generation Apple Pencil

The Apple Pencil detailed above supports either the iPad Air, or the 2020 iPad Pro.

If you have an iPad or iPad mini that was manufactured in 2020 or later, then you can use the original Apple Pencil to sketch and tap. It's not magnetic, so you'll need to pull the cap off then plug the Pencil into the charge port on your iPad, but the original Apple Pencil is just as fun and creative as the second generation.

How to use the Apple Pencil

Write, annotate, and draw with the innovative Apple Pencil...

Using the Apple Pencil to tap, annotate and draw, feels surprisingly natural. Think of writing on a notepad or a clipboard, and you'll get the idea. Nevertheless, there are some clever features built into the Apple Pencil that you might now know about, such as a dedicated toolbar, a double-tap, and the ability to draw perfect shapes...

How to enter text

Whenever you see a text box, such as the web address field in Safari, or the search box in Maps, tap on the field using your Apple Pencil, then use handwriting to enter text.

If you need extra space to write then don't worry about going outside of the field - your iPad will know that you're entering text using handwriting. As you finish each word, your iPad will automatically recognise it and enter it as text in the field that you selected.

The toolbar

A helpful toolbar will appear at the bottom of the screen whenever your use an Apple Pencil. If it gets in the way of something, then you can drag it to the side of the screen. You can also shrink to the toolbar to a small ellipse by tapping the options button on the right-side of the toolbar, then toggle **Auto-minimise** on. Here's a quick overview of each button:

1 Tap this button to undo what you just wrote.

2 Tap this to redo a change.

3 This opens the on-screen keyboard, letting you quickly type other than use handwriting.

4 Tap on this ellipse button to access further options for the toolbar.

Enter a space

If you'd like to add a space in-between words, **tap and hold** between words as you write. This can be helpful if your handwriting is small and the iPad is accidentally merging words.

Select text

To quickly select words or entire sentences, just **draw a circle** around them using the Apple Pencil.

Delete words

You can get rid of something you've written with the Apple Pencil by **scratching it out**.

Swap languages

Your iPad will automatically recognise whether you're writing in English or Chinese. This means you can change languages mid-sentence, and your iPad will automatically enter the correct text or symbols.

Select hand-written text

While writing with the Pencil in the Notes app, **tap and hold** on a word, and in the pop-up field which appears, select **Copy as Text**. You can then paste the text somewhere else on your iPad.

Draw perfect shapes

While using your Apple Pencil in the Notes app, draw the outline of a shape then hold for a second. Your iPad will automatically recognise what you've scribbled, then turn it into a perfect shape.

Customise double-tap

You can double-tap on the Apple Pencil to perform a number of actions:
- Switch between the current tool and the eraser.
- Switch between the current tool and the last used tool.
- Open the colour palette.

To choose one of these, open the **Settings** app, select **Apple Pencil**, then make a choice using the DOUBLE-TAP panel.

Smart Keyboard Folio

Type comfortably with a physical keyboard...

There's no denying that writing on the iPad is a great experience. The display is large enough to accommodate a full-sized keyboard, while Multi-Touch capabilities let you access accent keys, emoji's and even turn the keyboard into a giant trackpad. So why would you want to buy the Smart Keyboard?

Well, for one it enables you to see a full-screen view of your document, art, or work. That's because as soon as you attach the Smart Keyboard, your iPad automatically recognises it and turns off the on-screen keyboard. Second, the Smart Keyboard acts as a robust cover for your iPad, protecting the screen when not in use while also acting as a stand for propping up the device during a movie.

So how does it work? A highly-durable fabric is laser-ablated to form the shape of each key. This provides a spring-like tension which mimics the feel of a traditional key, while eliminating the need for traditional mechanisms. The fabric of the keyboard is water and stain-resistant, but only 4 millimeters thin to ensure the keyboard is slim and lightweight. Beneath the top layer is a conductive layer of fabric which reads each keystroke then seamlessly communicates each press back to the iPad. It does this instantly, and without the need for wires, so you can enjoy a simple yet technologically advanced way to type.

Shortcuts bar

When the Smart Keyboard is attached to your iPad, text-based apps such as Notes, Mail, and Pages automatically recognise the keyboard and offer a full-screen view of your work. However, look at the bottom of the screen and you'll see the shortcuts bar. You can use this to perform commands with the iPad, swap between apps, or access the search bar.

Keyboard shortcuts

While using a text-based app, hold down a key such as Command, Option, or Control, and you'll see which shortcuts work with the on-screen app. As an example, here are just a few of the shortcuts that work with Pages:

⌘ X = Cut
⌘ C = Copy
⌘ V = Paste
⌘ N = New Document
⌘ F = Search
⌘ D = Duplicate
⌘ shift W = Show Word Count
⌘ option C = Copy Style
⌘ option C = Paste Style

Magic Keyboard for iPad Pro

A full-sized keyboard with a laptop-like trackpad...

The Magic Keyboard is an amazing companion for your iPad Pro or 2020 iPad Air. It features the best typing experience ever on iPad, with a scissor mechanism keyboard, a trackpad that opens up new ways to work with iPadOS, a USB-C port for pass-through charging, and front and back protection. The Magic Keyboard also features a floating cantilever design, allowing you to attach iPad Pro magnetically and smoothly adjust it to the perfect viewing angle for you.

Compatible with:

- iPad Pro 12.9-inch (3rd and 4th generation)
- iPad Pro 11-inch (1st and 2nd generation)

Comfortable typing

Full-size, backlit keys ensure it's easy to type on the Magic Keyboard, even in the dark. The Magic Keyboard also features the same scissor mechanism found on the MacBook keyboard with 1 mm of travel, so typing is responsive yet quiet.

Floating cantilever design

The iPad appears to float over the Magic Keyboard, suspended in the air by the a cantilever mecahnism. The angle of the iPad can also be adjusted to ensure the perfect viewing angle is available.

Built-in trackpad

It's now possible to interact with your iPad Pro using gestures and a pointer, making it possible to easily select and manipulate text, spreadsheet cells, and more.

Front and back protection

The Magic Keyboard also acts as a protective case for both the front and the back of the iPad Pro.

How to use a trackpad or mouse

Use a pointer to select objects, manipulate text, and more...

The iPad has always been a versatile device for day-to-day tasks such as browsing the web and creating basic documents, but with a trackpad or mouse, it's pretty much a replacement for the traditional computer. That's because a trackpad or mouse makes it possible to easily select text, move objects, and even manipulate spreadsheet cells. Best of all, iPadOS supports a number of gestures which enable you to fully control every part of the iPad experience, using just the trackpad or mouse. To get started, it's recommended that you use one of these three accessories:

Magic Keyboard (for iPad Pro)

This full-sized keyboard includes scissor mechanism keys and a large Multi-Touch trackpad. It also includes a USB-C port for passthrough charging and front and back protection.

Magic Trackpad 2

Traditionally included with the iMac, this stand-alone trackpad can automatically connect to the iPad using Bluetooth.

Magic Mouse 2

Another accessory traditionally available for the Mac. If you've used a desktop computer in the past, then this will be a very familiar accessory to use with your iPad.

How to connect a Magic Trackpad or Mouse

To connect the Magic Trackpad or Mouse to the iPad, open the **Settings** app, tap **Bluetooth**, then select the accessory. If you don't see it, make sure to unpair it from your Mac first.

The basics of using the pointer

With a trackpad or mouse connected to your iPad, you'll see a circular pointer on the screen. This is called the pointer, and it moves around the screen as you slide your finger across the trackpad or move the mouse.

- **The pointer only appears when you need it.** The pointer isn't persistent at all times, instead only appearing when you're touching the trackpad or moving the mouse.

- **It can change shape based on what it's pointing at.** The pointer changes shape to be the size of the button or app below it, and if you move it over text, it turns into a thin vertical line. You can disable this by going to **Settings** > **Accessibility** > **Pointer Control**, then toggling **Pointer Animations** off.

Wake your iPad

You can wake up your iPad by using a trackpad or mouse. Just click it and you'll see your iPad wake up.

Unlock your iPad

Move the pointer to the Home bar at the bottom of the screen and you'll automatically unlock your iPad.

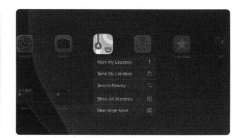

Right-click

You can right-click on apps, text, and objects to access the same secondary menu found when tapping and holding.

Return to the Home Screen

To go home using the trackpad, swipe up with three fingers. If using a mouse, move the pointer to the Home bar then click on it.

Access the Dock

To quickly access the Dock at anytime, move the pointer to the bottom of the screen.

Access Control Centre

To adjust settings or control music at any time, click the **status icons** in the upper-right corner to bring up Control Centre.

The multitasking screen

You can jump between apps or force-close them by swiping up and holding with three fingers.

Jump between apps

You can swipe between open apps by swiping left and right with three fingers.

Slide Over apps

Move the pointer over the Slide Over app, then swipe using three fingers to jump between apps.

Apps included with your iPad

Your iPad comes with all the apps you need for basic tasks...

App Store
Browse and install millions of apps for your iPad. If you can think of it, then there's probably an app for it.

Books
Buy, download, and read books from the Apple Books store.

Camera
Take photos and videos with your iPad.

Clock
Set alarms and see the time at various locations around the world.

Calendar
Add and view appointments, birthdays, and other reminders.

Contacts
Your very own phone book, where you can create and edit contacts.

FaceTime
Make free video calls to friends and family.

Files
Access all of the files, folders, and downloads on your iPad.

Find My
This app lets you locate all of your Apple devices that you own. You can also play alert sounds, send messages, and even remotely wipe them of your personal data.

Mail
Read and write emails.

Maps
View aerial or classic maps of the entire world. You can also get directions and information for businesses and places.

Messages
Send instant messages to friends and family.

Measure
A replacement for the common tape measure, letting you measure objects in the real world.

Music
Listen to music, podcasts, and audiobooks. You can subscribe to Apple Music through this app, which offers millions of tracks for a monthly subscription.

News
Read the latest news stories from various sources within your country.

Notes
A pocket notebook, where you can enter text, make lists, and even add tables.

Photos
View all of the photos and videos taken on your iPad. You can also share them, view them in albums, and view slideshows.

Reminders
Centered around your calendar entries and alerts. You can also input new reminders for events and alerts.

Safari
Browse and navigate the internet.

Settings
Access all the settings for your iPad, set restrictions, and customise notifications.

Shortcuts
With this app you can create custom commands for running tasks.

TV
Watch movies and TV shows from Apple and service providers within your country.

How to remove default apps

How to get rid of the apps you never use...

Even the staunchest Apple fan will admit that some of the default apps on iPad are unnecessary. After all, not everyone is a stock analyst, and we don't all use the Shortcuts app to create custom commands. It's possible to organise any unnecessary apps into a specific folder then forget about them, or alternatively, you can delete these apps and forget about them entirely. To do this simply tap and hold the app icon that you'd like to remove, then when it starts to wiggle tap the **X** button. You'll see a warning that any local data and app settings will be removed too. If you're happy to proceed tap **Remove** and the app will vanish from your screen.

Default apps you can remove...

- Reminders
- Stocks
- Calendar
- Contacts
- Facetime
- Find My
- Home
- Books
- iCloud Drive
- iTunes Store
- Mail
- Maps
- Music
- News
- Notes
- Podcasts

There are some downsides to removing default apps. For example, if you delete the Mail app then tap an email address within Safari, you'll see a pop-up window which suggests you restore the Mail app.

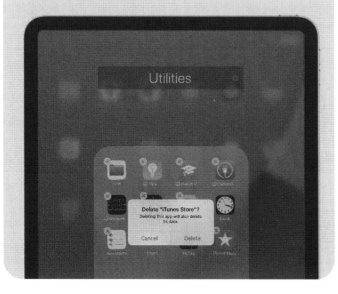

Restore a deleted default app

Wondering how you can restore a deleted app such as Notes, Stocks or Find Friends? It's easy, just open the **App Store**, search for the app you'd like to restore then tap the **iCloud** button. In an instant (remember these apps aren't actually deleted from your iPad) the app will be back on the Home Screen and ready to use.

Explore the App Store

Discover an unlimited number of amazing apps for your iPad...

Your iPad is a pretty amazing tablet straight from the box, with a great web browser, note-taking app and photo editor; but if you'd like to do something specific, such as watch Netflix, make a Zoom video call, or play a video game, then you'll need to visit the App Store where there are millions more apps to discover.

Think of the App Store as a shopping mall, but for apps. To find it, look for this icon:

Open the App Store, and it's hard not to be overwhelmed by the sheer number of apps, tools, and games available. You'll initially see highlighted apps for the day. This is curated by a team within Apple, and they usually handpick some of the most inventive and fun apps out there. Look at the bottom of the screen, and you'll see shortcuts to the latest games, apps, Apple Arcade (a subscription service focused around games), and a search shortcut which lets you look for a specific app.

How to install an app

To install an app, just tap the **GET** button if it's a free app, or the **price** button if it's a paid app.

After you've entered your Apple ID password, the app will be added to the Home screen of your iPad

Pocket Yoga
Rainfrog, LLC
£2.99

Back

Chess - Play & Lea
Chess.com

GET In-App Purchases

In-app Purchases

Wondering why that amazing-looking app is free? Chances are it has in-app purchases. These are optional purchases you can make within an app to unlock extea features. To see if an app includes in-app purchases, look for the text "In-App Purchases" next to the get/price button.

Data privacy

Many apps within the App Store will want to track you in various ways. Some will want to look through your contact information, while others might want to access your photos, or even your shopping history. You can see how an app tracks you by looking for it in the App Store, then scrolling down to the **App Privacy** section. From here you will see a breakdown of what the app does with your privacy. If you don't like what you see, then you can ignore the app and look for another.

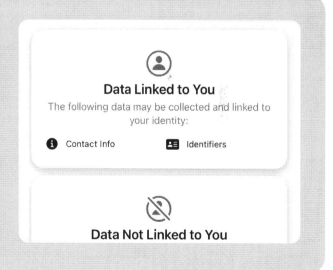

Data Linked to You
The following data may be collected and linked to your identity:

ⓘ Contact Info Identifiers

Data Not Linked to You

How to review an app

Want to tell others about how great (or terrible) an app is? First make sure you've already downloaded the app, then head over to its page on the App Store, scroll down to the **Reviews** section, then tap **Write a Review**.

Top social media apps

Keep in touch with friends and family...

With its large pin-sharp display, the iPad is a great way to make video calls to friends and family. It's also helpful for sharing photos and writing heartfelt messages to loved ones. To get you started, here are a few social media apps used by millions around the world. You can find them by opening the App Store then using the search feature:

Facebook
Social Networking
★★★☆☆ 46K

The number one social media platform in the world, Facebook is a great way to keep in touch with friends and family. It also has its very own marketplace for finding local bargains.

Messenger
Text, audio and video
Editors' Choice

You'll need a Facebook account to use Messenger, but once signed up, you can send messages to friends and family and even make free video calls.

Instagram
Photo & Video
★★★★★ 2.5M

Share photos and videos with others around the world. Where Instagram differs from other social media platforms is that it enables you to follow celebrities - not just your friends and family.

TikTok
Real People.
★★★★★ 627K

TikTok is focused entirely around short video clips, mostly themed around dance, lip-sync, comedy, and upcoming talent. With its focus on fast-paced entertainment, it's easily possible to lose an entire evening scrolling through silly video clips.

Pinterest
Healthy recipes
★★★★★ 345K

For the creative type, Pinterest can provide a continuous source of inspiration. It enables you to share and discover recipes, home ideas, artwork, style inspiration, and more.

Twitter
Live news
★★★★★ 433K

With a limit of just 280 characters, Twitter is focused entirely on efficient communication. It's used by presidents, businesses, celebrities, and regular folks alike, and stands alongside Facebook as one of the biggest social media networks on the planet.

LinkedIn
Network & Find Jobs
★★★★☆ 10K

Think of LinkedIn as a social media platform for careers. After creating a profile detailing your career and skills, you're able to search for jobs, and network with similar people.

Reddit
Find your community
★★★★★ 132K

One of the biggest, oldest, and most diverse communities on the web. Reddit is compromised of endless "subreddits", each focused around a subject such as Star Wars, Art, Memes, and more.

Top productivity apps

Edit a complex spreadsheet, create a short film and more...

It might have a handheld-sized screen, but it's still possible to edit spreadsheets and create presentations on the iPad. To get you started, here are a few apps focused around productivity and timekeeping...

Pages
Documents
★★★☆☆ 3.2K

Think of Pages as Microsoft Word, but it's made by Apple and is free for the iPad. Using Pages you can create documents and letters, and even open and edit Word files.

Keynote
presentations
★★★☆☆ 1.6K

Keynote is Apple's answer to Microsoft's Powerpoint, enabling you to create beautiful presentations and slideshows.

Numbers
spreadsheets
★★★☆☆ 1.3K

If you need to create spreadsheets on your iPad, then Numbers is the app of choice. It works surprisingly well on a touchscreen, while also being able to open Excel files.

Microsoft Office
Word, Excel
★★★★☆ 1.6K

There are individual apps available for the Microsoft Office Suite, but this takes the basics from each and combines them into a single app. You can open and edit Office files, create PDFs, and access your personal cloud storage.

Focus
Pomodoro
★★★★☆ 173

If you're a busy person juggling multiple jobs at once, then Focus will help you to perform at your best by splitting your work into multiple sessions.

Agenda.
Date-focused
★★★★★ 328

Agenda is a combination of a notepad, task manager and journal, but all based around date-focused tasks.

Grammarly
Type with confidence
★★★★☆ 2.3K

Grammarly is a professional text editor and spell checker, able to improve your writing and grammar in real-time. It will suggest alternative words, fix broken sentences, and generally help to improve anything you write.

Flow
Sketch. Think.
★★★★☆ 278

This was Apple's iPad app of the year in 2019, and it's easy to see why. Flow takes the legendary Moleskin notebook experience and brings it to life on the iPad, enabling you to create drawings, beautiful art, and notes.

Top utility apps

Check the weather, track your calorie intake and more...

The iPad is truly the pocket-knife of the 21st century, with the ability to become nearly any tool you need. Whether you're looking for an accurate weather forecast, want to know which stars and planets are overhead, or want to monitor your calorie intake, these are the best apps available...

 Dark Sky Weather
Weather
★★★★⯪ 11K

Get an accurate forecast of the rain to the exact minute, with Dark Sky for the iPad. It can give you a minute-by-minute, hour-by-hour, or weekly forecast. A helpful radar animation also helps you see where the rain is moving overhead.

 MyFitnessPal
Calorie Counter
★★★★⯪ 201K

If you're serious about losing weight, then MyFitnessPal enables you to build a daily diary of calorie intake by scanning the barcode on food and drink, track your weight over time, and set a daily calorie limit.

 SkyView®
Explore the Universe
★★★★⯪ 311

Simply point your iPad at the night sky, and this app will tell you precisely what planets, stars, satellites and constellations are in front of you.

 Airbnb
Holiday rentals
⁂ Editors' Choice ⁂

Look for unique hotels, experiences, and places to stay around the world. You'll never struggle to find somewhere interesting, with locations suitable for holidays and business trips alike.

 KAYAK Flights
Find the best travel price
★★★★★ 15K

Find cheap flights or hotels around the world with this travel-based app. What makes it stand out from similar apps is the ability to chain multiple flights together, but the ability to also book hotels and explore destinations really add to the experience.

 Google
The official Search
★★★★⯪ 33K

Yes, you can search Google using the Safari app on your iPad, but this dedicated app works faster, while also offering the ability to watch videos inside of search, use Google Lens, and translate text from one language to another in realtime.

 Tripadvisor
Trip Planner
★★★★⯪ 48K

With more than 700 million reviews from travellers around the world, the Tripadvisor app is a great way to find and compare hotels, restaurants and attractions.

 Shazam
Find songs
⁂ Editors' Choice ⁂

If there's a song playing in the background that you don't recognise, Shazam will identify it for you, then let you know where it can be purchased or streamed.

 Rightmove
Find properties
★★★★★ 18K

Whether you're looking to buy or rent a property, RightMove is the number one app of choice. Nearly every property on the market is listed here, and it's easy to filter search parameters based on price, location, and more.

Top shopping and food apps

Order takeaway food or shop for any item on earth...

If you're looking to shop, sell, find food or look for culinary inspiration, these iPad apps are all you need.

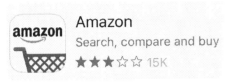

Amazon
Search, compare and buy
★★★☆☆ 15K

With the most significant digital store in the world, and the ability to buy nearly anything with a single tap, the Amazon app is an essential download for your iPad.

Apple Store
Shopping
★★★⯪☆ 4K

Not only can you purchase Apple products and accessories using this official app, but you can also book an educational session in one of its stores.

eBay
Buy, sell and save
★★★★★ 965K

The biggest auction site on the planet, eBay lets you bid, buy, or sell nearly anything you can imagine.

Etsy
Shop Handmade
★★★★★ 52K

Think of Etsy as the worlds number one shop for handmade and one-of-a-kind items. Using the app, you can shop for items, chat directly with shop owners, and get notifications.

Deliveroo
Order takeaway
★★★★⯪ 659K

Feeling hungry? The Deliveroo app is the perfect way to discover takeaway food in your area, order and pay for it, then track it in realtime as the delivery driver brings it to your door.

Yelp
Local food, Shopping
★★★⯪☆ 891

Using the Yelp app, you can search for restaurants in your area, check out the opening hours, menu, and even book a table.

ChefsFeed
The Expert Guide
★★★⯪☆ 5

If you're planning to stay in and cook for the night, ChefsFeed is a brilliant way to find inspiration. Using the app, you can take part in live interactive classes, discover recipes and ideas, or find the best restaurants and bars in your area.

Lush Cocktails
Food & Drink
★★★★☆ 5

With a massive selection of cocktail recipes, and a fun interface that includes animated liquid sloshes as you browse from drink to drink, Lush Cocktails is a great way to discover and create your very own cocktails.

Uber Eats
Restaurant Food
★★★★⯪ 180K

If you didn't find the right dish on Deliveroo, then Uber Eats is a good backup choice. It covers most large cities, and is often priced competitive with its rivals.

Top creativity apps

Create art, edit photos, or layout an app...

The iPad makes for the perfect canvas, able to simulate traditional brushes, clean vector lines, or even 3D models. Here is a selection of apps that will get your creative juices flowing...

 Procreate
Sketch, paint, create
Editors' Choice

An incredible app which enables you to paint or draw using realistic looking brushes. Procreate also supports layers and a powerful undo tool, plus the ability to export a timelapse video of your art coming to life.

 Pixelmator
Photo & Video
Editors' Choice

If you need to edit a photo with professional results, or even create a sketch or painting, then Pixelmator is a powerful tool built specifically for the iPad.

 AutoCAD
DWG Viewer & Editor
★★★★☆ 404

A commercial tool used to design and draft, this iPad iteration enables you to view, edit, and create CAD drawings on the go.

 Adobe Illustrator
Create Vector Art
★★★★⯪ 6.3K

Although not as powerful as the desktop version of Illustrator, this iPad version still enables you to create amazing illustrations using vector tools. With regular updates over time, it promises to become a powerful tool to match its desktop sibling.

 uMake - 3D CAD
Easy 3D Sketch
★★★★☆ 322

If you've ever wanted to dabble in 3D modeling, then uMake is a great place to start. After creating a 2D sketch, the app can automatically extract a 3D form out of it, enabling you to further tweak and edit as needed.

 Noteshelf
Note-Taking
★★★★☆ 160

If you prefer to sketch notes, rather than write them down, then Noteshelf is the app for you. It enables you to mix hand-drawn images, audio, plus text to create beautiful notes. You can also use the app to annotate PDFs.

 Adobe Comp
Productivity
★★★★☆ 124

Adobe Comp CC enables you to quickly build a wireframe layout, or even add basic shapes, images, and hotspots.

 Adobe Fresco
Drawing, painting
★★★★⯪ 814

Adobe Fresco attempts to replicate the art of painting by simulating paint thickness. You can even smudge the paint with your finger to blend colours and textures.

Top iPad games

Go racing, build a castle, or race your friends...

With a massive touchscreen and powerful GPU underneath its screen, the iPad makes for a genuinely great gaming device. From classic games such as Angry Birds and Minecraft, to full PC classics like Civilization, there's plenty of gaming choice in the App Store. Here are just a few of the best games on offer.

Asphalt 9
Arcade Car Racing
Editors' Choice

Featuring an extensive roster of real-life hypercars from Ferrari, Porsche, Lamborghini and more, this beautiful and fast-paced racing game is a joy to play on the iPad.

Angry Birds 2
Best arcade game!
Editors' Choice

This unique touch-based puzzle game is still one of the best. It tasks the player with destroying towers filled with green pigs. To do this they must use giant slingshots to fire angry birds through the air. Genius.

Fortnite
Battle Royale & Party
★★★★⯪ 666K

For a while this took over the competitve gaming world, with fast-paced first-person shooting action. It's still a blast to play, and with regular updates that change the virtual world, there's always something new to see and do.

Minecraft
Create, explore
Editors' Choice

Build literally anything you can imagine, or dig deep into the earth to mine precious resources, then craft weapons and armour to survive the hordes of monster which come out at night.

Monument Valley
A story of beauty
Editors' Choice

An absolutely beautiful puzzle game which challenges the player to guide a mother and her child through dozens of illusionary puzzles.

Civilization® VI
Build. Conquer.
★★★☆☆ 402

The full turn-based strategy game is now available on the iPad, and it works perfectly with touch controls. If you're looking for a time-sink game to fill a lot an afternoon, then this is the perfect choice.

Mario Kart Tour
Race around the world
★★★★★ 89K

It's Mario Kart - but on your iPad! Enjoy competitive racing along dozens of colourful tracks. With support for multiplayer racing, you can also test your skills against up to seven other players too.

Lara Croft GO
Breathtaking Puzzle A(
Editors' Choice

A turn-based adventure game which tasks the player with navigating lush environments and puzzles using simple swipe-to-move controls.

Use Safari to browse the web

Visit websites, organise tabs, customise your experience, and more...

Browsing the web using Safari on iPad is a wonderful experience. Websites look stunning on the large display, with crisp text and vivid images, and they load in an instant. Thanks to the all-new multitasking capabilities, it's also possible to browse the web while reading your emails, checking out the latest tweets or making a FaceTime call.

This chapter will explain how the Safari app works, how to take advantage of its features and how you can customise the experience to best suit your needs.

You'll find the Safari app already installed on your iPad. Just unlock your iPad then tap on this icon:

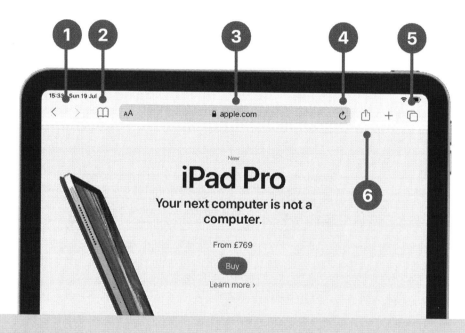

The basics

1 Use these arrows to go back a page, or forward a page.

2 Access your favourite websites and bookmarks by tapping this button.

3 Tap the **search** field to search the web or type a website address.

4 Tap this curved arrow to refresh the page. **Tap and hold** to view the desktop version of a site.

5 Tap the **Tabs** button to view all of the tabs open on your iPad.

6 Tap the **Share** button to send a webpage to another iPad, message a link, email a link, print the page and much more.

Visit a website

To visit a website, open **Safari**, then tap on the address field at the top of the screen. Next, enter the website's address, then tap the blue **Go** button on the keyboard.

Search the internet

The address bar in Safari also acts as a search engine, so to search the web for any question or search term, just type your query into the address bar at the top of the screen.

Use tabs to visit more than one website

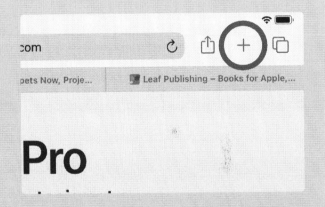

Think of a tab as a single view of a webpage. You can have as many tabs open on your iPad as you like, but you can only view one at a time.

To open a new tab view, press the **plus (+)** button at the top of the screen.

Explore, open and close tabs

To see an overview of all your tabs, tap the **tabs** button in the very top-right corner of the screen. To close a tab, press the small **X** button in it's top-left corner.

If you accidentally closed a tab and want to go back to it, press and hold the **plus** button (**+**) and after a second a pop-up window will appear showing your recently closed tabs.

Customise page settings

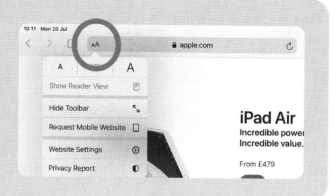

While viewing a website, tap the **AA** button next to the address bar to zoom the page, hide the toolbar, request the mobile version of a page, or adjust settings.

Search a web page

To find a piece of text on a webpage, tap the **Share** button in the upper right corner, then tap **Find on Page**. You can then use the keyboard to search the web page for text.

View two websites at the same time

While using Safari, bring the Dock up and drag the Safari icon to the side of the screen. You'll now open a second window, allowing you to browse two websites at once.

Translate a page

To translate a web page from French, Spanish, Simplified Chinese, German, Russian, or Brazilian Portuguese, to your own language, tap the **AA** button at the top of the screen, then choose **Translate to English**.

Add a bookmark

If you visit a website regularly then it's a good idea to bookmark it. This lets you easily re-visit the website by either opening a new tab, or by tapping the Bookmarks button at the bottom of the screen.

To add a new bookmark, tap the **Share** button at the top of the screen, then choose **Add Bookmark**.

View and manage your bookmarks

To quickly visit your bookmarks, tap the **Bookmarks** button in the upper left corner of the screen.

To remove or edit a Bookmark, swipe across it from right to left, then tap **Delete**.

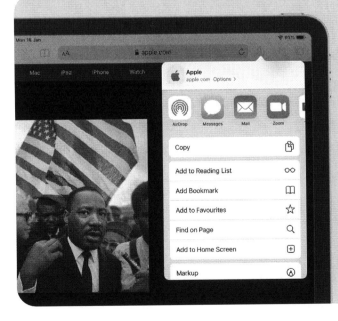

Share a website

Sometimes it's helpful to share a website with friends and family. Safari offers a wealth of sharing options, including the ability to email web pages, send a website like via the messages app, and much more.

To access these sharing abilities, tap the **Share** icon at the top of the screen. You'll see the share panel appear, with icons and shortcuts to each sharing ability. Tap on whichever is most suitable for your needs.

Send an email

Compose messages, organise your inbox, and more...

Alongside the Messages app, Mail must come close to being on the most used apps on iPad. That's because if you're serious about doing things on the web, like shopping or registering for services, then there's no way to avoid having an email address.

Thankfully, the Mail app on iPad is easy to use and gets straight to the point. It's designed with a clean, white interface that helps you focus on what's important: your emails. Buttons are coloured blue, and basic Multi-Touch gestures enable you to delete messages, flag them and more. You'll find the Mail app already installed on your iPad. To find it, just unlock your iPad then tap on this icon:

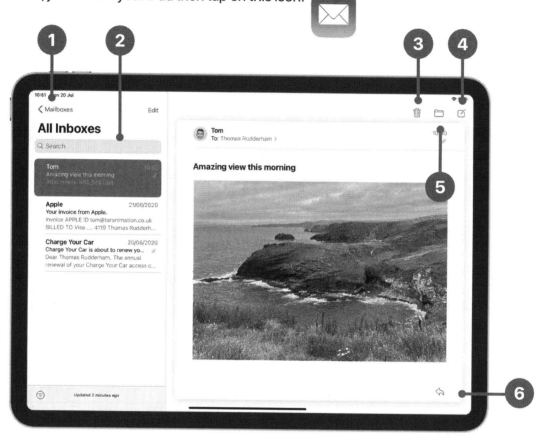

The basics

1 Use this back arrow to return to the Mailboxes screen, where you can access your Drafts, Sent, Junk, and Trash mailboxes.

2 Looking for a particular email or recipient? Pull the inbox down then use the **search box** to quickly find it.

3 Delete an email by tapping the **Trash** icon.

4 Tap this button to create a new email.

5 Tap this icon to move an email into a folder.

6 Reply, forward, flag, or print an email using this arrow button.

Send an email

When you're ready to send an email, tap the **new email** button in the very top right corner. You'll then see the compose window slide into view. Here's an overview of what each field does:

- **To**: In the field, type the email address of the person or organisation that you wish to email.
- **Cc**: In this field, enter the email addresses of people that you want to include, but are not addressing directly.
- **Bcc**: Anyone in this field will receive your email, but won't see the other email addresses of anyone else included in the message.
- **Subject**: Type a short title to describe your email.

When you're ready to send the email, tap the **blue arrow** in the top right corner.

Format text

If you'd like to bold, italicise or underline a word or sentence, highlight the text then tap on the **option** arrow. Next, tap **BIU** and select the format you wish to use.

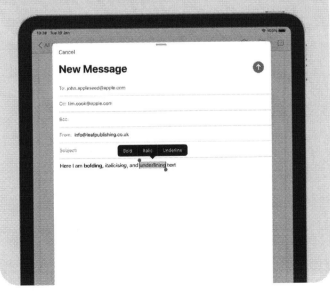

Attach images

To attach an image within an email, tap and hold where you want it to go, then tap the **camera** button above the keyboard. You can then decide whether to choose a photo from your library, or to take a photo on the spot.

Format text & sentences

Using the Mail app you can format text in a variety of ways, such as its colour, font style, and even paragraph layout. To do this, tap the **Aa** button above the keyboard to access a wide range of controls.

To change a specifc piece of text, select it by double tapping on it, then use the tools to change its appearance.

Scan and attach a document

When composing an email, it's possible to scan letters and documents, then attach them directly to a message. What's great is that scans actually look like scanned documents, thanks to some clever post-processing which straightens the image and fixes any white balance issues. To scan a document:

1 When composting an email, tap the **document** button above the keyboard, then choose **Scan Document**.

2 When the camera view appears, move it over the document you wish to scan and your iPad will automatically recognise it.

3 Take a photo, then adjust the corners of the scan to match the document.

4 Tap **Keep Scan** to save the image. You can continue to scan further documents, or tap **Save** to attach the image/s to your email.

5 The scan will now be attached to your email as an image.

Forward an email

To quickly forward an email to someone else, tap the **arrow** button in the bottom-right corner, then tap **Forward**.

Attach a drawing

You can attach a drawing to an email by tapping the **pencil** button above the keyboard. While drawing, you can choose from a variety of tools, such as a pencil, felt tip, marker, or ruler. You can further customise a tool by tapping on it, so tap on the felt tip tool and you'll be able to adjust the line thickness and opacity.

Swipe for options

Swipe your finger right-to-left across an email while in the Inbox, and you'll see a number of options appear:

- Tap **More** to reply, forward, mark, notify, or move an email.
- Tap **Flag** to add a coloured flag icon onto the email in your inbox.
- Tap **Bin** to delete the email.

Save a draft email

If you're composing an email and you're not ready to send it yet, drag the email down to the bottom of the screen. It'll stay there, below the rest of your emails, until you tap on it to continue the draft.

Chat using Messages

Send messages, photos, emojis, and even animated faces...

You might not think of the iPad as a device for sending messages, but that's exactly what you can do with the Messages app. For those times when your iPhone isn't to hand, it can prove to be a surprisingly fun and useful app, and because your messages are synced across all of your Apple devices, you can start a conversion on your iPad and continue it later on your iPhone.

To find the Messages app on your iPad, just look for the green app icon with a speech bubble:

The basics

1 Tap the **New Message** button to start a conversation.

2 Tap on a persons name or image to see more details about them.

3 Tap the **Camera** button to take a photo on the spot, or tap the **Photos** button to send an image from your library.

4 Tap and hold the **Microphone** button to send an audio message. Let go when you've finished recording.

5 Access a variety of characterful emojis by tapping this button.

6 If you need to move the cursor around, tap and hold on the **spacebar** to turn the keyboard into a trackpad.

Send a message

Open the Messages app, then tap the **New Message** icon in the upper left corner of the screen. It looks like a blue square with a pencil in it.

In the **To**: field, type the phone number of someone you know. If you have already added them to the Contacts app, then you can also type their name.

Once you've entered someone's details, tap the text entry field just above the keyboard, then type a message. Once you're ready to send, tap the **arrow** button above the keyboard.

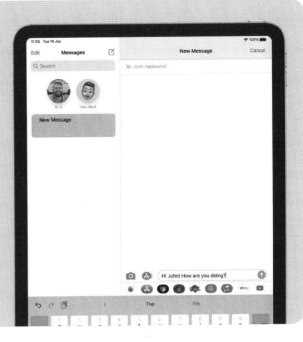

Send a photo

If you would like to send a photo or video to someone, then tap the **camera** button above the keyboard. You will see the Camera app open, which lets you take a photo on the spot.

If you would rather send a photo that you've already taken, then tap the **camera** button above the keyboard, then tap the small **album** button in the very top-left corner. You can then select a photo saved on your iPad.

Dictate a message

If you would prefer to dictate messages, rather than type them, then tap the **microphone** button at the bottom of the keyboard and say your message out loud.

As your iPad listens to your voice, it will enter the correct words one at a time. You can add punctuation by saying words like "comma", and "full stop". When you're ready to send the message, tap the **arrow** button.

Send a voice message

Using the Messages app, you can record a voice message and send it to someone. Think of it like like leaving a voicemail.

To do this, tap and hold the **voice message** button above the keyboard. It looks like a grey circle with white lines inside. As you hold down the button, say your voice message out loud. When you're finished, let go of the button, and you'll see the following controls appear:

- **Cancel**. Tap the small "**X**" button to cancel the voice message.
- **Play**. Tap the **play** button to hear your voice message.
- **Up Arrow.** Tap this button to send the voice message to the other person.

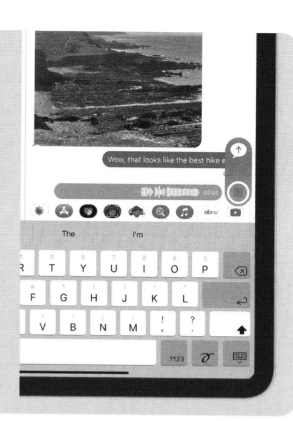

Delete a chat

There are two ways to remove chat conversations from the Messages app. The simplest is to **swipe right-to-left** across the chat conversation in the sidebar. Alternatively, tap the **Edit** button at the top of the Messages screen, select the conversation/s that you wish to delete, then tap the **Delete** button.

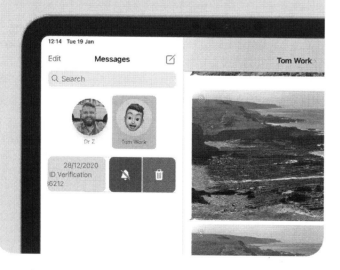

Pin contacts

If you talk to someone regularly, then it's a good idea to pin them to the top of the Messages home page. To do this, swipe across their chat conversation from left-to-right, then tap the yellow **pin** button. To remove them at a later date, simply tap and hold on their icon, then choose **Unpin**.

Send an emoji

To send an emoji, tap the **Emoji** button on the keyboard while composing a message. It's at the bottom of the screen next to the spacebar and microphone. You can swipe left and right to scroll through emoji's or tap the grey icons at the bottom of the screen to jump to an emoji category.

Send a handwritten note

Using the iPad's large display, you can write a handwritten note and send it using Messages. To do this tap the **handwriting** icon in the bottom-right corner of the keyboard, write your message, then tap Send. While handwriting a message you can also choose from a selection of preset messages by tapping the **timer** icon.

Automatically turn words into emoji's

So you've composed a message, but you want to liven it up with some fun emoji's. It's surprisingly easy, thanks to a clever feature that automatically scans your message for emoji-related words then lets you replace them with a tap. Here's how:

1 Compose a message with some emoji-friendly words (such as "happy", "fireworks", "pizza" etc).

2 Tap the **emoji** button on the keyboard. Any emoji-friendly words will glow gold.

3 Tap on the gold words that you'd like to replace and they will automatically swap from text to emoji graphics.

Send a quick sketch

With the Messages app you can draw a message and send it with just a few taps of your finger. Here's how it works:

1 When you're viewing or replying to a message, tap the **Digital Touch** button above the keyboard. It looks like two fingertips over a heart.

2 Start to draw on the black panel in the lower area of the screen. You'll see your drawing come to life.

3 Once you've finished tap the **blue arrow** icon to send the drawing.

It's not just a drawing you can send, there are five other effects including a heart beat and a fireball:

Taps

Simply tap anywhere on the black panel and an animated tap will appear.

Fireball

Press and hold on the screen with your finger. When you let go a fireball effect will be sent.

Kiss

Tap with two fingers and you'll send a kiss message.

Heartbeat

Tap and hold on the screen and an animated heartbeat will be sent.

Broken Heart

Tap and hold with two fingers then slide downwards to send a broken heart.

Send a message with an animated effect

If you'd like to emphasise a message with an animated effect then four hidden effects are included within the Messages app: a slam dunk, a loud shout, gentle whisper, or invisible ink. To do this:

1 Compose your text, then instead of tapping the blue send arrow, **tap and hold** on it.

2 In the pop-up window, tap one of the four options on the right-side of the screen to see a preview of how it looks.

3 Once you're happy with an effect, tap the **blue arrow** to send the message.

Search messages

You can quickly look through all of your messages to find contacts, links, photos, and even words from within a conversation. To do this, pull the sidebar down to reveal a search bar. Tap on this and you'll be able find recent contacts, links, photos, and search through message content.

Share your location

Meeting a friend somewhere in town? If they're having trouble finding you, tap on their **name** at the top of the screen, choose **Info**, then tap the **Send My Location** button.

Send a full-screen effect

Want to really grab someone's attention with a message? Try sending a full-screen effect. With the Messages app you can include one of nine effects that take over the screen for a brief moment. Here's how it works:

1. Compose your text, then instead of tapping the blue send arrow, **tap and hold** on it.

2. Tap the **Screen** tab at the top of the screen, then select an effect by swiping to across the screen with your finger.

3. Once you've found an effect tap the **blue arrow** button to send the message.

Manage your calendar

Learn how to add events and manage multiple calendars...

The calendar app on your iPad is surprisingly powerful. It can juggle multiple events throughout your day, factor in the time it takes to travel from one event to another, and even automatically block out chunks of time when you're on the road.

To find the Calendar app, simply search for it or look for this icon:

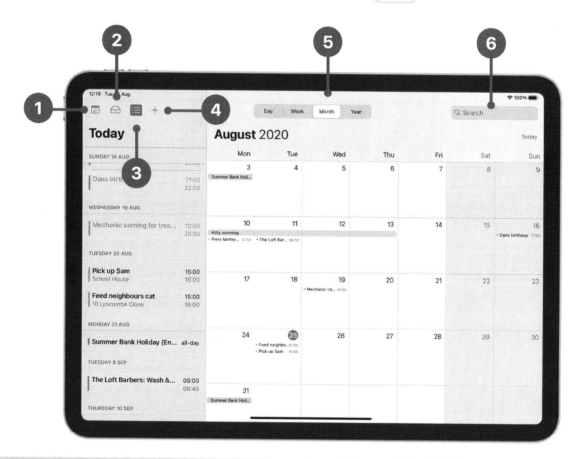

The basics

1 Tap the Calendars button to toggle individual calendars on or off.

2 Tap the Inbox button to accept calendar event invites, and see the replies you've sent.

3 Tap the sidebar button to show or hide the sidebar,

4 By tapping the **plus** button, you can add a new event to the calendar. See across the page for more on this.

5 Toggle between day, week, month, and year views using these tabbed buttons.

6 Tap on the **search** button to look for a specific event, such as a birthday, hotel booking, or public holiday.

Add a calendar event

1 Tap the **plus** button in the top-left corner.

2 Give the event a name by tapping on **Title**.

3 If the event takes place at a location, then tap the grey **Location** text to search for a place.

4 Tap **Repeat** if you'd like the event to occur every day, week, bi-weekly, month, or year.

5 You can ask the Calendar app to automatically factor in travel time, then block out your calendar for the duration of the trip. To do this tap **Travel Time**.

6 Tap **Invitees** to invite people to share the calendar event with you.

7 Tap the **Add** button when you're ready to add the event to your calendar.

If you're busy, use Day view

By using the Day view you can easily see detailed information for the day ahead. You can also jump from week to week by swiping through the days near the top of the screen.

Choose the default calendar

If you're the primary scheduler for a family or work calendar, then it's helpful to make that specific calendar the default choice. To do this go to **Settings** > **Calendar** > **Default Calendar**.

Get automatic alerts

If you'd like to be automatically reminded of birthdays and events before they happen, go to **Settings** > **Calendar** > **Default Alert Times**.

Tap for details

By tapping on an event you can easily delete it or view the location on a map.

Add an event with Siri

To quickly add an event to your calendar, initiate Siri then say something like "*add a calendar event to pick up Sam at 6 PM*".

Add a new calendar

If you'd like to create a calendar for specific events, tap the **Calendars** button at the top of the screen then tap **Add Calendar**.

Make a FaceTime video call

Make a free video call to friends and family using FaceTime...

With FaceTime, you can be with friends and family at any time and place. Whether it's a birthday, anniversary, meeting, or just a chat, FaceTime lets you be a part of the moment with crystal clear video and audio.

FaceTime works over both Wi-Fi or a cellular connection, and enables you to call another iPad, iPhone, iPod touch, or a Mac. It works like a phone call, but it's free, supports video, and you can even add realtime visual effects.

You'll find the FaceTime app already installed on your iPad. To find it, just tap on this icon:

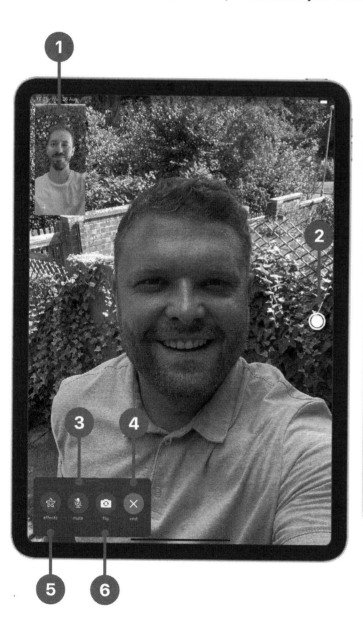

The basics

1 You can move the preview image of yourself around the screen by dragging it with your finger.

2 Take a photo of the conversation using this white button. Keep in mind that the other person will see a message to let them you've taken a photo.

3 Mute your microphone using this button.

4 End the call using this button.

5 Tap the **Effects** button to apply a wide range of filters, shapes, and video effects.

6 Flip your camera around using this button to show what's behind your iPad.

Make a FaceTime call

Open the FaceTime app and if you've used it before, then you'll see a list of recent contacts running down the side of the screen. Tap on one and you'll immediately call them.

If you've never used FaceTime before, then open the app, tap the blue **plus** button in the top right corner, then start to type the name of someone you know. As you type, your iPad will try and guess the correct person. Once they appear, tap on their name to call them.

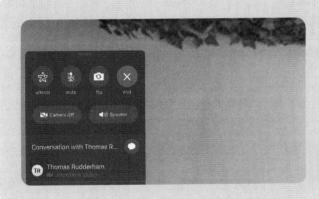

Access additional controls

During a FaceTime call, drag the **lower panel upwards** to access additional controls, including the ability to disable your camera, or begin a chat conversation.

Tips for making a great FaceTime call:

✓ FaceTime calls are completely free.

✓ You can only FaceTime someone who has an iPhone, iPad, or Mac.

✓ Make sure the other person can see you. It's easy to forget where the camera is pointing, so use the small preview image to check your appearance.

✓ The microphone is located on the top of your iPad, so if the other person says they can't hear you, make sure your fingers aren't covering the top half of the device.

✓ Turn your iPad on its side during a call, and the other person will see more of the room around you.

✓ You can invite up to 32 people to join your FaceTime call. To do this, pull the bottom panel upwards (see Access additional controls above), then tap the **Add Person** button. Enter their name into the **To** field, then tap the green **Add Person to FaceTime** button to invite them.

Take amazing photos

Get to know the camera app and all of its features...

The iPad might not be the first choice of camera for many, but that hasn't stopped millions of people from capturing magical moments and memories on the spot. The latest iPads continues that tradition, with a 12-megapixel camera that's capable of taking beautiful photos, can capture 4K video, and even film in slow motion. Additionally, the front-facing FaceTime camera is great for making video calls or taking a fun selfie.

Helping you to capture these moments is the Camera app. It's simple and intuitive to use, yet offers so many possibilities. To find the Camera app, just look for this icon:

The basics

1 Manually zoom in or out using the vertical slider on the left-side of the screen. On an iPad Pro tap the **1X** button instead.

2 Toggle Live Photo mode on or off by using this button.

3 Tap this button to set a timer.

4 If you have an iPad Pro, then tap this button to enable / disable the camera flash.

5 Swap between the front or back facing cameras.

6 Take a photo, or tap and hold to capture a Burst Mode photo.

7 Jump to your most recently taking photo by tapping this thumbnail image.

8 You can swap between camera modes by swiping or tapping the shortcut buttons here.

Take a photo from the Lock Screen

The quickest way to open the Camera app is via the lock screen of your iPad. To do this, just **swipe the Lock Screen from right-to-left** and the Camera viewfinder will appear.

Use the volume buttons

It's possible to take a photo by pressing the **volume up or down** buttons on the side of your iPad. This is especially useful for taking selfies with your arm outstretched.

Zoom even further

You can zoom up to 5x digitally by using the slider on the left side of the screen. You can also pinch your fingers on the viewfinder to zoom in or out.

Camera focus

The camera will automatically focus onto a prominent object or area of light, but if you need to manually focus the camera, just tap on the area or subject you wish to focus on.

Lock the focus and aperture

To lock the focus and aperture levels, **tap and hold** on a subject or area. After a second or two a flashing yellow box beneath your finger will indicate that the camera focus has been locked.

Take a Portrait Photo with iPad Pro

Portrait photos are amazing. They mimic a DSLR camera by blurring the background behind a person. To do this your iPad Pro uses machine learning to automatically detect the face and hair of a subject, the distance between them and the background, then it blurs the background to create a beautiful 3D effect. To use Portrait mode:

1 Open the **Camera** app and select **Portrait** mode.

2 Place the subject at least 2 feet away. If they are too close the Camera app will let you know.

3 Tap the **capture** button to take the photo.

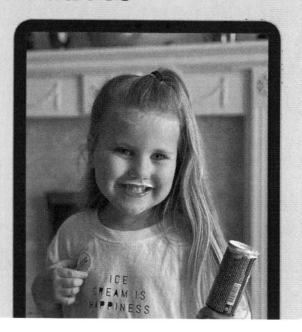

Use Portrait Lighting to take amazing selfies

By using Portrait Lighting mode you can simulate a number of professional photography effects and tools, such as a gold bounce card, to create even more beautiful looking photos. There are six effects to choose from:

Natural Light	**Studio Light**	**Contour Light**	**Stage Light**	**Stage Light Mono**	**High-Key Mono**
Your subject's face in sharp focus against a blurred background.	A clean look with your subject's face brightly lit.	Adds subtle shadows and highlights to the subject's face.	Your subject's face is spotlit against a deep black background.	Like Stage Light, but in black and white.	Adds a beautiful monochromatic effect.

To enable Portrait Lighting mode, open the **Camera** app and select **Portrait**. You'll see five buttons appear towards the bottom of the screen: Natural Light, Studio Light, Contour Light, Stage Light and Stage Light Mono. Select an effect by swiping through the options. Watch the screen to see the effect apply to your face in real-time. Press the **capture** button to take a photo.

You can choose another effect, even after the photo has been saved, by tapping the **Edit** button within the Photos app.

Shoot a video

Capturing video is easy, just swipe your finger across the camera viewfinder until **VIDEO** is centered, then tap the **red** button.

Film in slo-mo

One of the most fun camera features included with the iPad is the ability to shoot video in slow motion at 240 frames per second. It's great for capturing fast-moving objects.

While in the Camera app, swipe the text at the bottom or side of the screen until **SLO-MO** is centred. Next, tap the red record button to start filming your slow-motion video.

Edit a slow-mo video

To edit the slow-motion parts of a video, open the video in the **Photos** app, then tap the **Edit** button.

You'll notice a timeline at the bottom of the screen that's broken up by thin white lines. In the centre the lines are spaced further apart. This is the part of the clip which plays back in slow motion.

You can lengthen or shorten this slow motion part of the clip by dragging the white handles, then preview the clip by tapping the **play** button.

How to use the Camera timer

To enable the timer, open the **Camera** app and look for a **timer** icon just above the photo button. Tap it and you'll see three text options appear: **Off**, **3s** and **10s**. These correspond to the timer settings, so off is the standard setting, 3s gives you three seconds to pose, and 10s gives you 10 seconds to prepare yourself. Tap whichever you need, then tap the **Camera** button to snap a photo. You'll see a countdown appear on-screen and the camera flash will also emit a brief light for each passing second. After the countdown has ended your iPad will quickly capture 10 photos in a second. This stack of photos will be saved in the Photos app.

To pick a favourite, open the stack and tap the blue **Select...** text. Next, swipe through the images then tap the image (or images) you wish to save. Once you're happy with the selection, tap the **Done** button.

Capture time-lapse video

Have you ever wanted to capture a sun set, the changing tides, or the movement of clouds? Using the Camera app you can do this with the time-lapse feature. It works by capturing multiple photos, instead of video, over a period of time.

To capture a time-lapse video, open the **Camera** app, then select **TIME-LAPSE**. Next, place your iPad in a suitable location. Make sure it's steady – any movements over time will ruin the time-lapse effect. When you're ready, tap the **red record** button. Leave your iPad for a few moments or minutes - the longer the better - then tap the red record button again to end the time-lapse.

Capture a panoramic shot

Have you ever wanted to capture an incredibly beautiful vista? By using the PANO mode you can do just this by taking a super-wide, 180-degree photo.

PANO mode works by taking one very wide continuous photo. As you rotate on the spot, the camera captures the image as it appears on the right side of the lens. If there's any movement in front of you (such as people walking by), then you might see a few visual errors, but for vistas and still scenes the PANO mode works wonders.

1 Open the **Camera** app and select **PANO** mode.

2 You'll see a thumbnail in the centre of the screen with a white arrow pointing right.

3 Tap the **Camera** button at the bottom of the screen to start capturing a panoramic shot.

4 Slowly pan your device to the right. Keep a steady hand — if you wobble too much black bars will appear at the top and bottom of the photo.

5 Tap the **thumbnail** in the bottom corner to check out your panoramic image.

View and edit your Photos

Learn how to view, organise, and edit your photos...

The Photos app is a portal to your memories. Stored within its colourful icon are hundreds, if not thousands of treasured photos and videos. Photos of yapping dogs, family members, stunning landscapes, unflattering selfies, and treasured holidays. This is one of those apps that you're going to be opening on a day-to-day basis, so keep it somewhere prominent on the Home screen where you can quickly tap it.

Open the app, and you'll discover a clean, tidy interface that appears to be basic and easy to use. In many ways it is, but dig a little deeper, and you'll find one of the most productive and in-depth apps available for the iPad. With just one fingertip it's possible to edit photos, create albums, move and delete images, view memories, and much more.

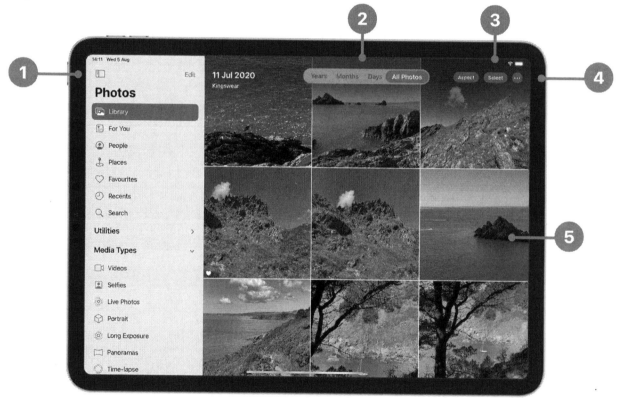

The basics

1 Whenever you want to browse your photo libraries, albums, and media types, tap the **sidebar** icon in the top-right corner. If you don't see the icon then swipe inwards from the left side of the screen.

2 View your photo library as individual photos, or grouped by days, months, and years using these tabs at the top of the screen.

3 Select multiple photos using this button.

4 Tap the **options** button to zoom in or out, adjust the aspect ratio, filter photos, or view them on a map.

5 Tap and hold on a photo to copy it, select it, share it, favourite it, or delete it.

All Photos

When viewing **All Photos**, you'll see a nearly endless grid of photos scrolling upwards and off the screen. You can scroll through them and tap on an image to see it bigger, or you can pinch to zoom in or out to see your photos spread over a wider range of time.

Days

Tap on the **Days** tab and you'll see a beautiful grid of images representing a single day. The Photos app intelligently organises your images, hiding duplicates while selecting a highlighted image or video.

Months

The **Months** view organises the most meaningful events into groups, then displays them as individual cards in a scrollable panel. The app tries to intelligently select the best photo or video to remind you of what the event was about. Think of it as a greatest hit library of your memories.

Years

Years gives you a high-level overview of your photo library, but what makes this view really special is it's dynamic and based on context. So open the Years view on your birthday and you'll see photos from your birthday celebrations going back as far as your photo library extends.

For You

Notice the **For You** option in the sidebar. Tap this and you'll be presented with albums of images that are organised into events, subjects, and highlights.

Every day a new set of albums and images will appear. Tap on an album to see more photos, the date they were taken, where they were taken, and related albums.

Albums

Scroll down the sidebar and you'll see a collection of albums called **My Albums**. These are based on:

- Albums you've created
- People and places
- Videos and selfies
- Live Photos and Portrait Photos
- Panoramas
- Time-lapse videos and slo-mo videos
- Burst mode photos
- Screen recordings
- Animated photos
- RAW images from a DSLR or iPhone 12 Pro

Create an album

To create a new album, tap on **All Albums** in the sidebar, tap the blue **plus** icon at the top of the screen, then choose **New Album**. Enter a title for the album then tap the **Save** button.

A window will then appear displaying all of the photos on your iPad. Tap the images you'd like to add to the new Album, then tap **Done** to save the new album.

Rename an album

While viewing the Albums screen, tap the **Edit** button. Tap on the title of the album and the keyboard will slide up the screen. Update or change the album name, then tap the **Done** button.

Move an image from one album to another

To move an image from one album to another, select an image then tap the **Share** button. In the pop-up panel, choose **Add to Album**, then select the album you wish to copy the image too.

Delete an album

From the Albums screen, tap the **Edit** button in the top-right corner. Small red buttons will appear alongside any albums you've created. Tap any of these and the album will be deleted from your iPad.

Look at people and places

Located in the sidebar are two buttons: **People**, and **Places**. Tap on **People** to see albums of friends and family that appear within your photos, or choose **Places** to explore a map of the world where your photos are placed in the correct location.

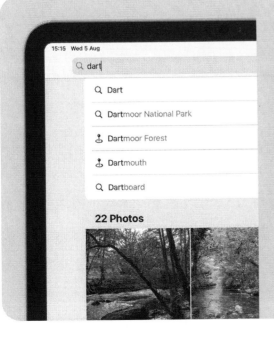

Search your photos

The Photos app can recognise objects, faces and locations, then automatically organise groups of images into albums. This clever form of visual recognition has another benefit: intelligent searching. To search for something in an image, tap the **Search** button in the sidebar.

Search for *"California"* and you'll see all your photos of California. You can be even more specific. So search for *"Trees in California"* and the Photos app will automatically show photos of trees within California. You can try other queries such as *"Tom eating pizza"*, or *"Sarah riding a horse"* and the Photos app will instantly present you with the correct results.

Share a photo or video

Open an image or video, then tap the **Share** button in the bottom left corner (it looks like a blue box with an arrow pointing upwards). You can send a photo or video to a contact at the top of the panel, or send it via email, Messages, AirDrop and more using the shortcut buttons.

Edit a photo

To improve the look of a photo, open an image in the Photos app, then tap the **Edit** button in the top-right corner. You'll see the screen darken, and a number of editing tools appear:

1 Tap the **ellipse** button to add markup to an image.

2 Tap **Done** when you're finished editing.

3 Pinch to zoom on an image while editing to get a closer look.

4 Tap the **Live Photo** button to disable the live effect, choose a different Live Photo still, or to mute the Live Photo footage.

5 Tap the **Adjustment Tools** button to access the editing tools.

6 Choose from a variety of photo filters.

7 Crop and rotate an image by tapping this button.

8 Select and work with editing tool by scrolling through this horizontal list.

How to add a filter

While editing a photo, tap the **Filters** button (it looks like three overlapping circles) at the bottom of the screen. You'll see ten filter options appear at the bottom of the screen. You can swipe through these to select one, then use the slider below to increase or decrease the filter effect.

Tap **Done** when you're happy with the filter and want to save it.

Crop or rotate an image

While editing a photo, tap the **Crop** button (it looks like a square with curved arrows around it) at the bottom of the screen.

To crop a photo, drag the edges of the photo inwards. If you crop too much, then you can pinch on the image with two fingers to zoom out. You can also choose from a range of aspect ratio sizes (such as widescreen or tall), by tapping the ratio button in the top right corner (it looks like three overlapping rectangles).

To rotate an image, drag the horizontal slider at the bottom of the screen. As you drag it left or right, you'll see the photo above rotate. A thin grid of lines will also appear, which is helpful for aligning objects or the horizon.

When you've finished making changes, tap the yellow **Done** button in the bottom right corner, and the photo will be saved.

Trim and edit videos

Open a video, tap the **Edit** button, and you'll find the same image editing tools that we discussed on the previous page. All of these tools enable you to adjust the light and colour of a video, rotate or crop it, and even add filters.

You can also trim the beginning and end of a video to adjust its timing and length. To do this, tap **Edit** then make a note of the timeline which appears just above the editing tools. By dragging the handles on each side of the timeline you can adjust the start and end points of the video.

How to delete photos

While viewing an image, tap the blue **Trash** button in the bottom-right corner of the screen, then choose **Delete Photo** in the pop up window.

The photo isn't immediately deleted. Instead, it's moved to a folder within the Albums section called Recently Deleted. There it will sit for 30 days, until it is finally deleted for good.

Favourite an image

Tap the **heart** button at the top of the screen and the image will be added to the **Favourites** album - which you can always access from the sidebar.

Select images

To select multiple photos at once, make sure you're viewing a collection of images (such as an album) then tap the **Select** button in the top-right corner of the screen. Next, tap the images you want to select. You'll see small blue circles with a tick appear over them.

Once you've selected all the images you need, use the controls at the bottom of the screen to share or delete them.

Use a photo as your iPad wallpaper

You can use any photo in your library as a wallpaper, which appears on both the Lock Screen and Home Screen of your iPad.

To do this, find the image you want to use, then tap the **Share** button in the bottom left corner. Next, scroll down and tap on the option called **Use as Wallpaper**.

Edit Live Photos

Live Photos are like the magical moving photos you might have seen in the Harry Potter movies, but they work with your photos. It's also possible to trim the video snippets before or after the photo, select a new keyframe, disable the audio or even change the visual effect animation of the Live photo. Read on to find out how...

Select a new key frame

If you've taken an action shot and noticed that the exact moment you wanted to capture is in the moving segment of the Live Photo, then you can easily edit the photo and select the exact frame as your key photo. To do this open the photo, tap the **Edit** button, tap the **Live Photo** button, then use the timeline scrubber to choose the new key frame.

Trim a Live Photo

Sometimes you might want to trim a part of the Live Photo effect. For example, maybe you suddenly moved the camera at the very last second.

To get started, select the photo, tap the **Edit** button, then tap the **Live Photo** button. Next, use the handles on either side of the timeline scrubber to fine-tune the start or endpoints. **123**

Listen to Music

Listen to your favourite tracks and albums on Apple Music...

The Music app has always been the best way to listen to music on iPad. It has a beautiful interface, access to millions of tracks via Apple Music, exclusive TV shows, curated playlists, videos, top charts, and Music 1.

There's a limitless source of music available in Apple Music, but it comes at a price: to access the full service you'll need to pay a monthly subscription. It's priced slightly differently for each country but roughly works out about the same as a large takeaway pizza. For anyone who listens to the latest charts, streams music on a daily basis or has a wide variety of music tastes, it's definitely worth the asking price. For everyone else, Apple Music still offers Music 1, the ability to follow artists and preview music.

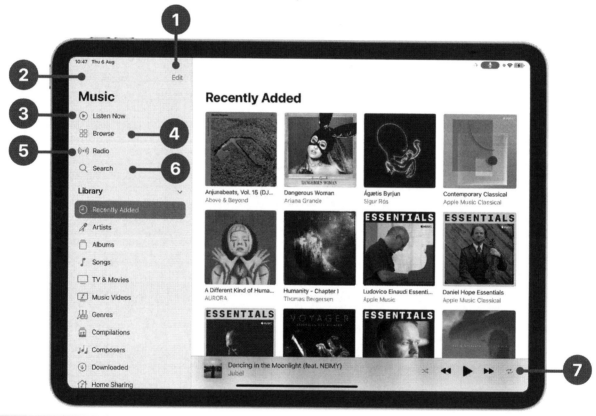

The basics

1 Tap **Edit** to genres of music from your Library, or to re-order items.

2 Use the sidebar to navigate through your library and explore Apple Music.

3 Tap **Listen Now** to see playlists created by Apple which suit your tastes, your listening history, what friends are listening too, and new releases.

4 Tap **Browse** and you'll find the latest tracks, top charts, music videos, and TV shows exclusive to Apple Music.

5 Tap **Radio** to discover a wide range of radio stations for every taste.

6 Tap **Search** to find songs, albums, artists, or lyrics. Either saved on your iPad or on Apple Music.

7 While a song is playing, tap on this panel to access playback controls.

Apple Music

To sign up for Apple Music, open the app and then tap the **Browse** button at the bottom of the screen. You'll then see a colourful banner which lets you sign up through the app.

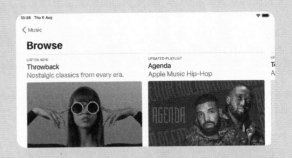

Search for music

If you're looking for an artist, song, album, or even lyrics, then tap the **Search** button in the sidebar. You can use the tabs near the top of the screen to search through both Apple Music and music saved within your library.

Add music to your library

If you see a track or album in Apple Music that you would like to save to your library, then tap the **+Add** button at the top of the screen.

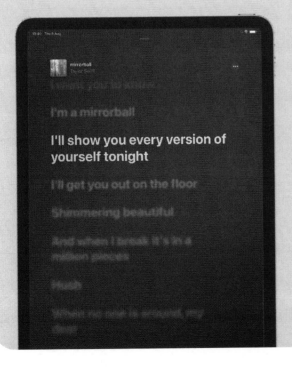

View music lyrics

Have you ever struggled to understand the lyrics of a song as it plays in the background? Using the Music app you see fullscreen lyrics for all your favourite songs, similar to karaoke.

When listening to a song, tap on playback control panel at the bottom of the screen, then tap the lyrics button in the bottom-right corner of the screen. It looks like a small speech bubble. You'll then see a fullscreen lyrics view take over. If you don't see the **lyrics** button, just make sure you're looking at the music playback window. You can get to it at any moment by opening the Music app then tapping on the small album artwork thumbnail at the bottom of the screen.

Shuffle music

If you're bored of an album track order, tap **Shuffle** and you'll never know what song is coming up next.

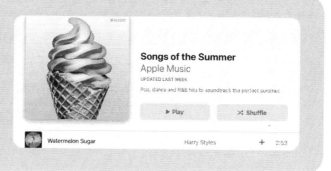

Delete a track or album

Fed up with a song or album? Just **tap and hold** on the track name or album artwork, then tap **Delete from Library**.

Add a Music widget to the Home Screen

By adding a Music widget to the Home Screen you can quickly jump to a recent song or album.

1 On the Home Screen, **tap and hold** in an empty part of the screen.

2 When all the apps start to wiggle, tap the **plus (+)** icon in the top-left corner.

3 Scroll down, then tap on **Music**. Select a widget size, then tap **+ Add Widget**.

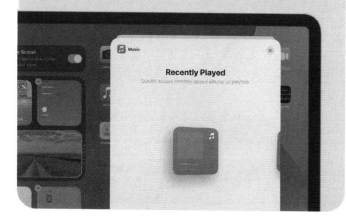

Automatically play similar music

If you're listening to a style of music and don't want it to end, then your iPad can automatically look for similar tracks and albums after the current one has finished.

1 While listening to music, tap the **list** button (≡) in the lower corner.

2 Next, tap the **loop** button (∞) which appears near the top of the screen.

3 Your iPad will automatically look for similar music.

Create a Playlist

Think of a playlist as your very own custom album, one with as many tracks and artists as you like. To create a new playlist of your own, open the sidebar, scroll all the way down, then tap **New Playlist**.

Add music to a playlist

To add a track or album to your new playlist, search for it in either your music library or Apple Music, then **tap and hold** on it. In the pop-up window, choose **Add to a Playlist...** The track or album will then be added to your playlist.

Listen to the radio

Tap **Radio** in the sidebar to listen to Apple Music 1, radio stations from around the country, or bespoke stations that are automatically compiled around your listening history.

See the top charts

What to see what's number one in the charts? Tap **Browse** in the sidebar, scroll all the way down then tap **Charts**. To listen to a track, simply tap on it.

Watch TV & Movies

Never miss an episode of your favourite show with this helpful app...

With so many sources of video content, subscription services, and streaming neworks, it has become difficult to keep track of the latest episodes of your favorite TV shows. Thankfully, the Apple TV app for iPad makes it a little bit easier, by collating many of the latest releases into one app. It also houses any TV shows or movies which you've purchased on iTunes, and remembers where you last left off.

To find the Apple TV app on your iPad, just search for it using Spotlight, or look for this icon:

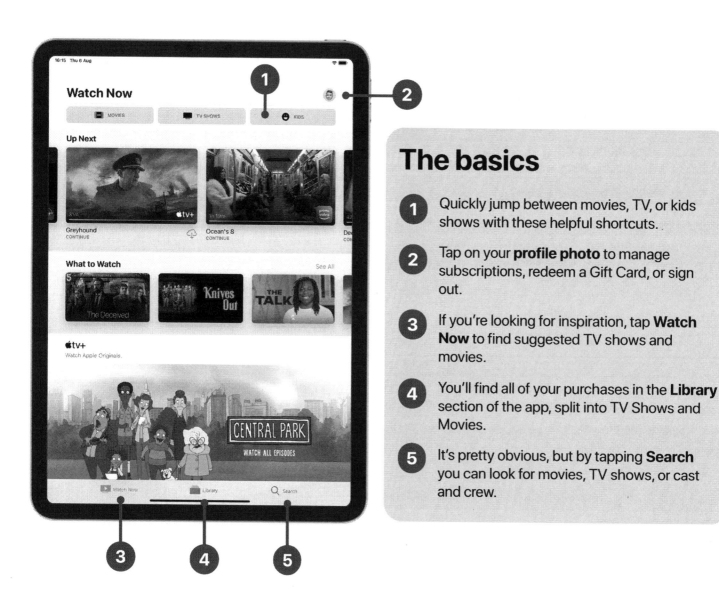

The basics

1. Quickly jump between movies, TV, or kids shows with these helpful shortcuts.

2. Tap on your **profile photo** to manage subscriptions, redeem a Gift Card, or sign out.

3. If you're looking for inspiration, tap **Watch Now** to find suggested TV shows and movies.

4. You'll find all of your purchases in the **Library** section of the app, split into TV Shows and Movies.

5. It's pretty obvious, but by tapping **Search** you can look for movies, TV shows, or cast and crew.

Toggle audio and subtitles

While watching a video, tap the **speech** icon next to the playback timer to toggle different audio sources or subtitles.

Access special features

If you've rented or purchased a movie with special features, then watch the movie in landscape mode. You'll see buttons for special features appear along the bottom of the screen.

Download a film

If you want to save a purchased film to your iPad, tap on its **artwork**, then tap the **iCloud** button.

Action & Adventure · 2017 · 2 hrs 13 min

Spider-Man [Tom Holland] begins to navigate his new identity as the web-slinging super hero under the watchful eye of his mentor Tony Stark.

▶ Play

Find out more about cast

Search for an actor, producer, director, or other member of crew, and you can see what films they've been in, created, or made a guest appearance.

Purchase Music, TV, & Movies

Purchase media and download it straight to your iPad...

There are still a large number of people who prefer to purchase and own their favourite albums, TV shows, and movies. That's where the iTunes app comes in. It contains nearly every song ever released, alongside millions of movies and popular TV shows. Once a piece of media has been purchased, it can be downloaded and saved to your iPad, and it will always be yours to keep.

To find the iTunes app on your iPad, look for this icon:

The basics

1. Search for artists, songs, movies, or cast and crew.

2. Tap the **share** button to send an album, movie, or TV show via email or message.

3. Purchase an entire album by tapping this button. If you have already purchased a track, then the price will have reduced.

4. Tap on a song to preview it, or tap the price button to purchase the track.

5. Jump between music, movies, TV shows, the Top Charts, Genius suggestions, and past purchases using these buttons.

Preview a track

While viewing an album, tap on a track to hear a preview. You'll hear a 30-second preview for songs less than 90 seconds in length, and a 90-second preview for longer tracks.

Download to your iPad

Once you've purchased something from the iTunes Store, it will automatically download to your iPad.

To find your purchases, tap the **Purchased** button at the bottom of the screen.

Genuis suggestions

As you make purchases over time, iTunes learns what music and video content you like. Eventually it will offer purcahse suggestions, which you can find by tapping **Genius** at the bottom of the screen.

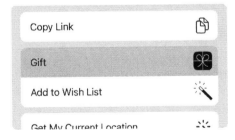

Gift songs, shows, & films

While viewing something in the iTunes app, tap the **share** button in the top-right corner, then choose **Gift**. You can then choose who to send it too and make the payment.

The Wish List

To save an item to your Wish List, tap the **share** button, then choose **Add to Wish List**. To view your Wish List, tap on **Music, Movies** or **TV Shows**, then tap **List** in the top-right corner.

Redeem a gift card

If you have received an iTunes gift card, tap on **Music**, scroll to the bottom of the screen then tap **Redeem**.

Take part in a workout class

Try yoga, dance, and core exercises...

Fitness+ is a new subscription service from Apple, focused on workout classes that you can do from home. It's rather like a VHS/DVD workout tape, but because Fitness+ combines both your iPad and Apple Watch, you can see your progress and heart rate in realtime. New classes are added daily too, so there's always something new to try.

Fitness+ offers 10 different workouts types, including: High Intensity Interval Training (HIIT), Strength, Yoga, Dance, Core, Cycling, Treadmill (for running and walking), Rowing, and Mindful Cooldown. The service also learns what you like, and monitors your progress, then recommends workouts based on what you enjoy doing.

To find the Fitness+ service, open the Fitness app on your iPad. Its app icon looks like this:

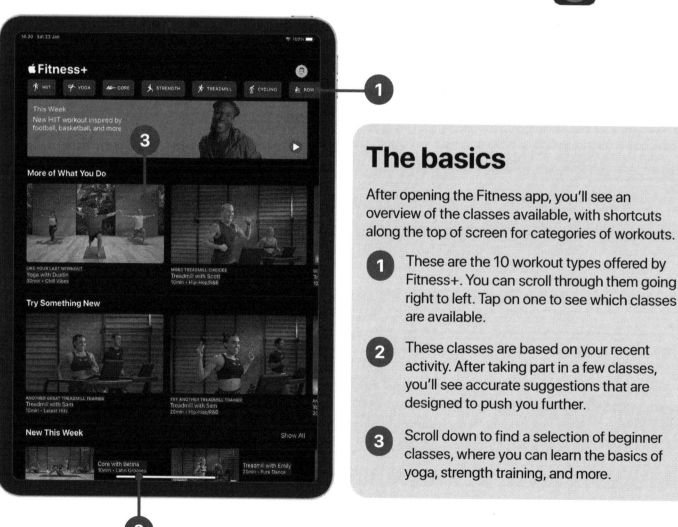

The basics

After opening the Fitness app, you'll see an overview of the classes available, with shortcuts along the top of screen for categories of workouts.

1 These are the 10 workout types offered by Fitness+. You can scroll through them going right to left. Tap on one to see which classes are available.

2 These classes are based on your recent activity. After taking part in a few classes, you'll see accurate suggestions that are designed to push you further.

3 Scroll down to find a selection of beginner classes, where you can learn the basics of yoga, strength training, and more.

Use an Apple Watch

Fitness+ works best if you're wearing an Apple Watch. This allows the app to track your heart rate and movements, with two benefits:

1. You can accurately track your calories as the class progresses. These will appear both on your Apple Watch, and on your iPad.

2. You can pause and play the class using your Apple Watch.

Pick a class

After finding a class on the Fitness+ screen, tap on it to find out more. You'll see how long the class lasts, can take a look at a short preview, begin the class, and see what music tracks are used in the background.

Yoga with Jessica

Take part in a class

Once you begin a class, you'll see a trainer appear on-screen alongside two assistants. As the class progresses, you'll see your heart rate and total calories appear in the top-left corner. Over in the right corner, you'll see your fitness activity rings for the entire day so far. Watch as they slowly close during the class. If you decide to end a class early, tap on the screen then tap the **pause** button, or use your Apple Watch.

Use Maps to navigate the world

Discover new places, get route guidance, and more...

With a map of the entire globe in your iPad, it's no longer possible to get lost in a busy city or strange new land. That's exactly what the Maps app gives you, alongside directions, real-time traffic information, transit timetables, 3D views of major cities and more. All of this for free and fully accessible at any time.

To find the Map app, just unlock your iPad then tap on this icon:

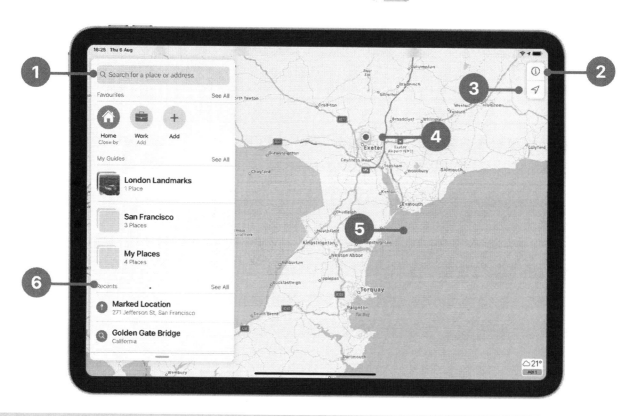

The basics

1 Tap on the **search field** to search for a place, address, or landmark.

2 Tap the **Info** button to change the view, toggle traffic, or mark your location.

3 Tap this blue arrow to move the map to your current location.

4 This blue dot represents your current location in the world.

5 This is the main map view. You can pan and zoom using your fingers.

6 Notice the information panel on the side of the screen. This automatically displays your recent activity, so you might see how long it will take to get home, where your car is parked, or where an event in your calendar is happening. You'll also find any collections of places you've saved alongside recently viewed locations.

Swap view modes

When you open the Maps app, you'll see the world in a 2D vector mode. If you'd like to view satellite imagery instead, tap tap the **i** button in the top right corner, then choose **Satellite** in the panel which slides up the screen.

View live traffic

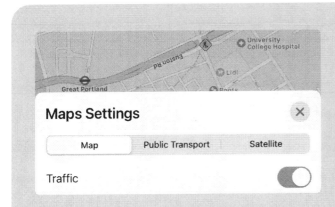

If you're planning a road trip, then it's a good idea to see how busy the route ahead is. To see live traffic on the map view, tap the **i** button in the top right corner, then make sure **Traffic** is toggled on. You will then see coloured lines appear on the road to indicate traffic. Green represents flowing traffic, orange means slow, while red means very slow.

Explore what's nearby

To find local business and places of interest, tap on the search field in the upper left corner, then use the various icons to see what's nearby. Scroll down, and you'll also find articles and guides to nearby cities.

Call a business or place of interest

If you're exploring the map and find a local business or place of interest, tap on it to find out more. You might see TripAdvisor reviews, photos, opening times, phone numbers, and useful pieces of information.

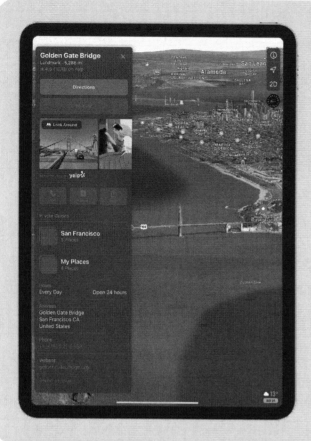

See a 3D map

Using the Maps app it's possible to navigate the world's most famous cities in beautiful 3D graphics. To view the 3D map, ensure you're in satellite mode, then zoom in on the map. When you're close to the ground, you'll notice a **3D** button appear in the upper-right corner. Tap it and the Maps view will tilt, then load a 3D landscape with detailed 3D buildings.

To rotate the image, simply place two fingers on the screen then rotate them. To tilt the camera, simultaneously move two fingers up or down the screen. Moving them left or right will pan the camera.

Look Around in first-person

Look Around mode lets you explore the world at street level using 360-degree imagery. It's almost like you're walking down the street itself, and it offers an incredible way to explore the cities of the world.

To use the Look Around mode, zoom the map until you see a binocular icon appear in the top-right corner. At the time of writing, it will only appear in major cities within the United States. Once you see it, tap the icon and Look Around mode will begin.

To pan the view, just push it with your finger. To move in any direction, double-tap where you want to go. You can also tap on a tag to see more information about the place or business.

Enjoy a flyover tour

Want to enjoy a 3D tour of a city? Simply search for the city's name, then tap the **Flyover** button in the information panel. You'll then be treated to a 3D tour of the city. You can pause it as you go, then use your iPad to look around.

Search indoor maps

With the Maps app you can find your way around airports and shopping centres using the indoor maps feature, which displays the locations of stores, rest rooms, and more. Most international airports and major shopping malls are fully mapped. Just look for a "Look Inside" badge that appears beneath the name of the airport or mall. When you see it, tap **Look Inside**.

See Transit information

If you're exploring a location using public transport then it's a good idea to view the local area using the Transit view in Maps. This lets you see nearby train stations, tube lines, bus stations, taxi pick-up points and more.

To enable this view simply tap the **Info** icon in the top-right corner of the screen then choose **Public Transport**.

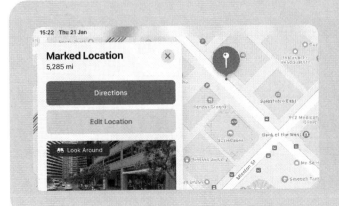

Drop a pin to learn more

To see detailed information about a specific point, simply **tap and hold** your finger on the screen and a pin will be dropped underneath it. Tap on that pin and you'll see more information about the location, including its address and distance.

Search Maps using Siri

If you'd rather search for a place or person using Siri, hold down the **Power** button (or Home button on a regular iPad) until Siri appears, then say something like "*where is the nearest hotel?*"

Turn-by-turn navigation

Satellite navigation and GPS technology have made driving to unfamiliar locations so much easier; and with an iPad, you can take advantage of this same technology to explore and navigate the world. It's wonderfully easy to use. Once set up, Maps will display the route in 3D, with road signs and written directions. And if the traffic conditions change, Maps will offer an alternative route for you to take.

1 To get started, open Maps then tap the **Search** field in the information panel. Next, enter the destination you wish the navigate to. This can be an address, zip code, or you can tap and hold on the map to drop a pin.

2 Once you've searched for an address, tap the blue **Directions** button to enable turn-by-turn instructions. Maps will automatically find the optimal route to the destination. It will also offer alternative routes, if any are available, which appear as opaque blue lines on the map. You can tap on these alternative routes to choose them.

3 Once you've found a suitable route tap the green **GO** button to begin following turn-by-turn directions.

Maps will automatically speak directions out-loud when you approach turns, lane changes, and exits - just as you'd expect if using a dedicated Sat-Nav device. You can even press the **Power** button to turn off your iPad display and it will light up whenever a change in direction is needed.

Adjust voice commands

To turn off the Siri voice commands pull the information panel upwards from the bottom of the screen, tap the **Audio** button then select the relevant option.

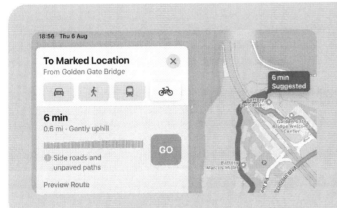

Get Walking or cycling directions

If you're planning a route on foot or a bike, then use the small graphical buttons to select either walking or cycling directions. If going by bike, then you can plan a route that avoids hills and busy roads.

Report an issue with the map

To report an error or missing place, tap the **Info** button in the top-right corner of the screen then tap **Report an Issue**.

Create and edit Notes

Learn how to quickly jot down notes, plus much more...

At first glance, the Notes app is a fairly basic way to jot down ideas and lists. It's much more than that, however. With the Notes app you can collaborate with friends, draw and annotate, scan documents, format text, create tables, and more.

To find the Notes app, just look for this icon on the home screen of your iPad:

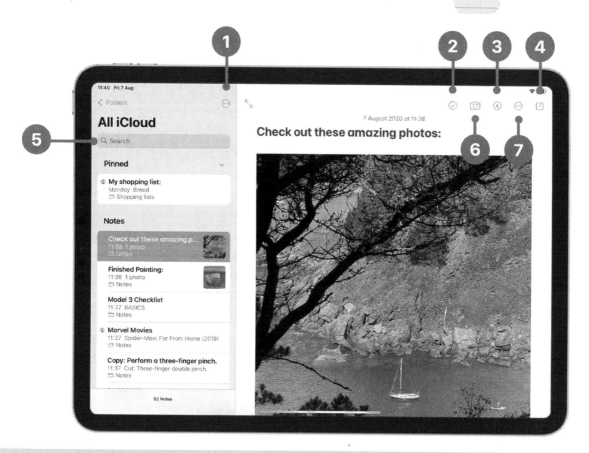

The basics

1 Tap the **options** button in the sidebar to toggle views, select multiple notes, or view attachments.

2 Create a checklist of items by tapping the **tick** icon.

3 Add a hand-drawn sketch to a note by tapping the **pencil** button.

4 Create a new note by tapping this button.

5 You can search for notes, words, and attachments by tapping on the **search** field.

6 Tap the camera button to attach a photo within a note. You can also scan documents using this button (see over the page for more on this).

7 While viewing a note, tap the **options** button in the top-right corner to share it, move the note, add a grid background, or delete it.

Create a new note

To create a new Note, open the **Notes** app, then tap the **New Note** button in the top-right corner. A blank note will then slide into view, and you can begin typing straight away.

Sketch in a note

If you'd like to draw into a note, tap the **pencil** button in the top-right corner. A sketchpad will now appear on-screen, enabling you to draw with a pen, felt tip or pencil. You can change the colour of the line by tapping the **small black circle**.

Add bulleted lists

If you're making a list of items (such as a shopping list), then you can create bulleted lists and check them off one by one.

To do this, write the first item on the list, then tap the **tick** button above the keyboard. To add a second item press the return key. To mark items as complete, tap the circle to the left of the item.

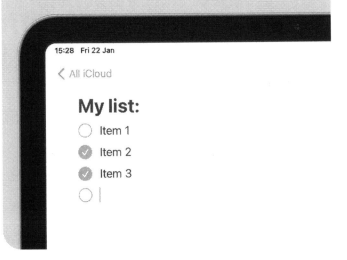

Insert a photo

Tap the **camera** icon at the top of the screen and three options will appear:
Choose Photo or Video. This enables you to insert a photo saved on your iPad.
Take Photo or Video. This lets you take a photo on the spot.
Scan Documents. Turn the page for more details on this feature.

Scan a document

Using the notes app, it's possible to scan letters and documents, then attach them directly to a note. What's great is that scans actually look like scanned documents, thanks to some clever post-processing which straightens the image and fixes any white balance issues. To scan a document:

1 While viewing a note, tap the **camera** icon at the top of the screen.

2 Select the **Scan Documents** option.

3 When the camera view appears, move it over the document you wish to scan and your iPad will automatically recognise it.

4 Tap **Keep Scan** to save the image. You can continue to scan further documents, or tap **Save** to attach the image/s to your notes.

5 The scan will now be attached to your note as an image.

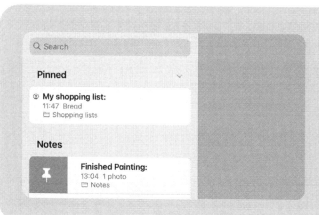

Pin a note

While viewing a note, tap the **options** button in the top corner then choose **Pin**. The note will then be pinned at the top of the sidebar, making it easier to find.

Create a table

Start by creating or opening a note, tap where you want to insert the table, then tap the **table** icon just above the keyboard. You'll then see a 2-by-2 table appear.

To add content to a row or column, tap on it then use the keyboard to enter text. To add additional rows or columns, tap the buttons above or to the left of the table.

Search for a note

To find a specific note, open the sidebar then tap on the **search** field. You can search for keywords or use the suggestions below to filter note types.

Add a grid background

You can add a variety of grid-based backgrounds to a note. To do this tap the **options** button, then select **Lines & Grids**. On the following panel you can choose a style.

Delete a note

From the overview screen of the Notes app, **tap and hold** on the note you wish to remove, then tap **Delete**. You can also swipe across a note in the sidebar then tap the **Delete** button.

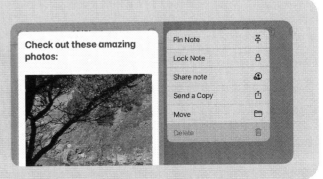

Create Reminders

Set yourself reminders so you'll never forget a thing...

The iPad already includes a notes app that can be used to jot down ideas and thoughts, but Reminders makes it easy to create to-do lists, set deadlines, and organise your life. It can also remind you with alerts at pre-determined times.

That's not all the app does, of course. It can group reminders into categories and even automatically sync reminders across all your devices via iCloud.

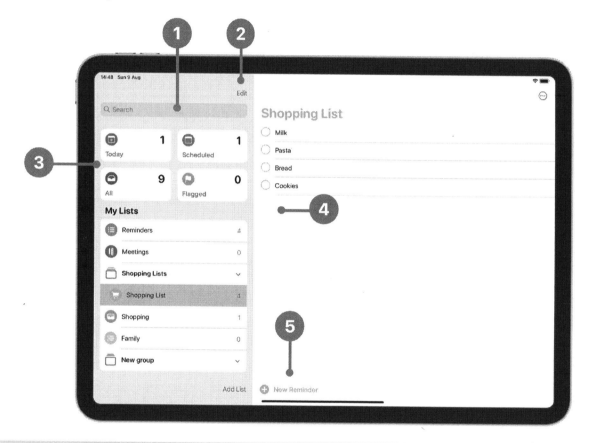

The basics

1 Search for reminders, lists, or list items using the search bar at the top of the screen.

2 You can rearrange or delete entire lists by tapping the **Edit** button.

3 Select a reminder or list here. You can also rearrange items by tapping, holding, then dragging.

4 You can quickly add additional items to a reminder list by pressing the **Enter** key.

5 To create a brand new reminder list, tap the **Add List** button in the bottom-left corner.

Create a new Reminder

From the home screen of the Reminders app, tap the **Reminders** option under My Lists, then tap **New Reminder** in the bottom corner. Give it a name, then tap **Done**.

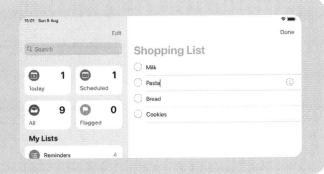

Date and time reminder

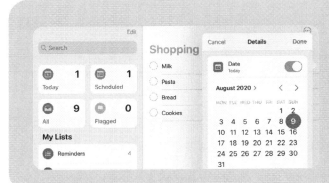

To remind yourself to do something at a specific date and time, tap on the new reminder, then tap the **i** button. In the pop-up window, toggle **Date** and **Time** on, then set a day and specific time if necessary.

Set a location reminder

Similarly, you can also remind yourself when you reach a location. To do this toggle **Location**, then either enter an address or choose from one of the suggested options.

Mark a reminder as complete

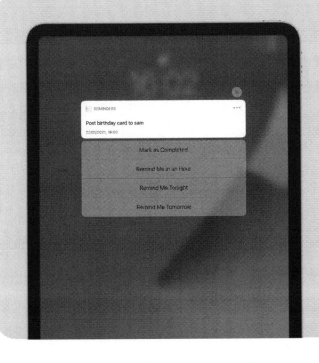

When a reminder is due, your iPad will let you know in two ways:

1 If your iPad is locked, you'll see a notification on the Lock Screen.

2 If you're using the iPad, you'll see a notification appear at the top of the screen.

To dismiss this reminder, tap and hold on it, then tap **Mark as Completed**. You can also adjust the reminder to alert you at a future time.

Create a group of reminders

From the home screen of the Reminders app, tap **Edit** in the top corner, then **Add Group**. Give the group a name then tap **Create**. You can now drag and drop reminders into this group.

Create a subtask

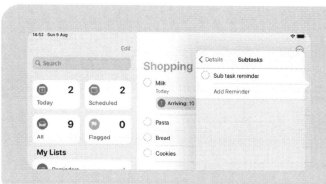

You can add a subtask to more complex reminders or lists. To do this tap on the reminder, tap the **i** button, then scroll down and choose **Subtasks**. Tap on it and then hit **Add Reminder** to add a subtask.

Delete reminders

From the home screen of the Reminders app, slide a reminder towards the left then tap the red **trash** icon to delete it. You can delete multiple lists and reminders by tapping **Edit** in the top-right corner.

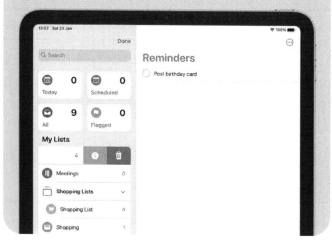

Create a reminder using Siri

You can add reminders by using Siri. Just hold the **Power** button (or the **Home** button on a regular uPad), then say something like *"Remind me to pick up Sam"*. Siri will then automatically create a new reminder.

Share a reminder

To share a reminder or list with someone else, tap on the Reminder or list, tap the **options** button in the top-right corner, then choose **Share List**. You can then send an invitation to someone via Messages, Mail, WhatsApp, and even Facebook.

When you share a reminder or list, you can do the following:
- View, edit and delete the reminder or list
- Mark items as complete, or add and delete items
- See, add and delete other people
- Stop sharing the list
- Delete the list

People you have shared a reminder or list can:
- View and edit the lis
- Mark items as complete, or add and delete items
- See who else is sharing the list

To stop sharing a reminder or list, tap **Edit** in the upper right corner, tap **Sharing**, then swipe to the left over any person you wish to remove. Tap **Done** when you're finished.

Assign a colour and icon

You can customise reminders and lists to make them easier to distinguise from each other.

To do this, slide a reminder or list towards the left then tap the **info** button. In the pop-up window, you'll be able to re-name the reminder, assign a colour and give it a unique icon.

147

Manage your Files

Discover how to manage files stored on your iPad and in Cloud...

If you've ever used a desktop computer or laptop, then you'll feel at home using the Files app. It's basically a Finder app for the iPad, letting you organise, edit, and delete files across all of your Apple devices and cloud services.

Open the Files app and you'll see the Browse screen, with shortcuts to search through your files, browse iCloud Drive, see local files on your iPad, and access any cloud-based services you have, such as Dropbox.

Files open or work in different ways depending on their file type. For example, images can be previewed, edited and marked up from within the Files app, while zip files can be previewed, but you can't extract their contents.

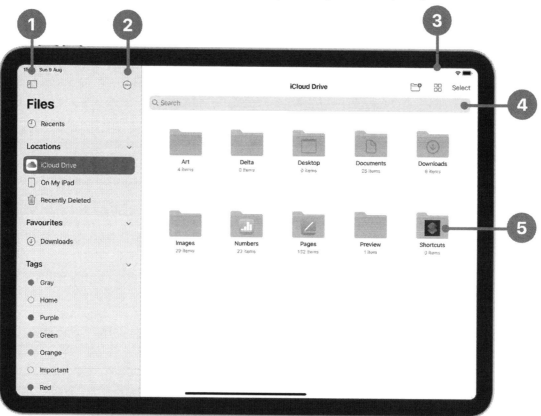

The basics

1 You can minimise the sidebar at any time by tapping this button.

2 Tap the **options** button in the sidebar to scan a document, connect to a server, or edit the sidebar contents.

3 Tap the **Icons** button in the top-right corner to change the view layout of a folder.

4 Search for a file on your iPad or within iCloud using this search field.

5 Tap and hold on a folder or file to copy, duplicate, rename, move, or delete it.

Toggle views

If you want to fit more things onto the screen, tap the **Icons** button in the upper-right corner of the screen, then choose **List**. You can also use the **Icons** button to sort your files by name, date, size, or tag colour.

Tap and hold for more options

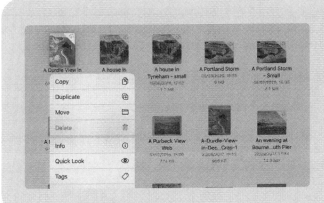

You can **tap and hold** on both folders and files to copy/duplicate/delete them, see more info, add a tag, favourite them and even compress/uncompress them.

Create a folder

By creating a folder, you can easily organise your files into tidy collections. To create a folder, tap the **New Folder** button in the upper-left corner, then use the keyboard to give it a new. Tap the blue **enter** key when you've finished.

Move a file into a folder

To move a file into your new folder, tap the **Select** button at the top of the screen, then tap on the file/s that you want to move. Next, **tap and hold** on the files you've just selected, then drag them into the new folder with your finger.

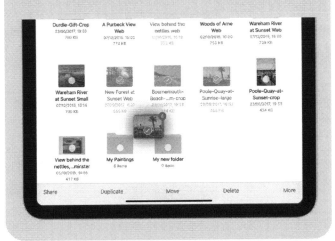

An overview of the Settings app

Get to know the basics of Settings...

Whenever you want to make a change to your iPad, adjust a setting, or update the operating system, then the Settings app is the place to go.

You can easily find the Settings app by looking for the icon with a cog gear in the centre:

Open the Settings app and you'll see a list of shortcuts to all the important settings on your iPad. They're labelled logically, so if you want to adjust how apps notify you, then tap on the Notifications shortcut. Similarly, if you want to connect to a new Wi-Fi network, tap Wi-Fi.

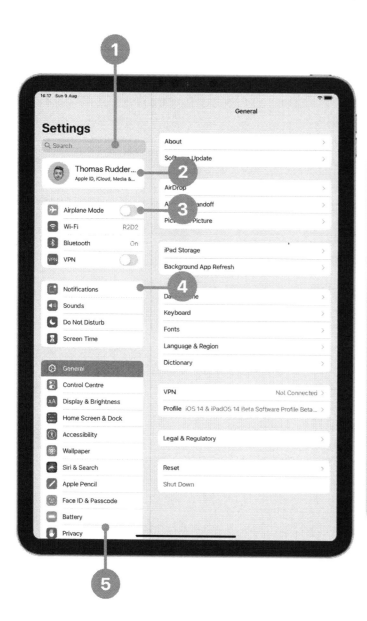

The basics

1 Search for individual settings using the search bar. If you don't see it, then pull the sidebar downwards using your finger.

2 Tap on your profile to access your Apple ID, where you can modify iCloud, iTunes, and device settings.

3 Enable Airplane mode from here if you're boarding an aircraft, or need to save battery.

4 Configure notifications from this shortcut. Other shortcuts from the Settings home screen include accessibility settings, Siri settings, and more.

5 Scroll the sidebar downwards to access additional settings, including individual app settings.

Search through Settings

The Settings app is packed with toggle switches, fields, and features for customising how your iPad works. Many are hidden away in sub-sections that you probably wouldn't find unless you were really determined, so if you need to quickly change a setting, open the **Settings** app and drag the sidebar down. A search bar will appear, enabling you to quickly find a setting or switch.

Find individual app settings

To access individual app settings, open **Settings** then scroll down. Keep going and you'll find individual app settings. You can also search for an app by using the search box.

Check for updates

If you'd like to check for the latest system update, go to **Settings** > **General** > **Software Update**. If an update is available, tap on it, enter your passcode, then either set a schedule or update straight away.

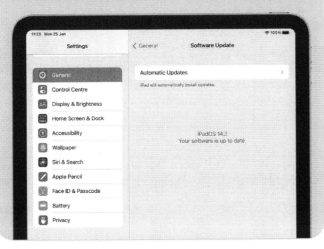

Change the wallpaper

Changing the background wallpaper is a great way to freshen the look and feel of your device. It's easy to do, just open the **Settings** app, tap **Wallpaper,** then **Choose a New Wallpaper**.

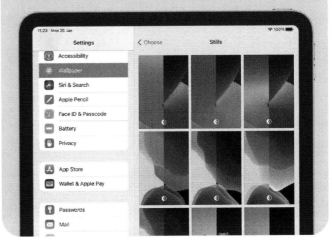

Adjust volume settings

Open the **Settings** app and choose **Sounds**, and you'll see a number of audio options appear. The slider near the top of the screen enables you to alter the volume level, while toggle buttons let you turn vibrations on or off.

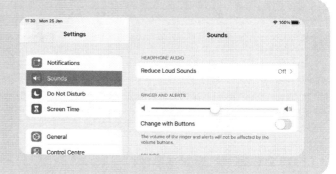

Change a text or ringtone alert

From the same **Sounds** panel, notice the options below the volume slider. These enable you to choose from a wide variety of ringtone alert effects. Choose an option (such as **Text Tone**), then tap on a sound effect to preview and select it.

Protect your hearing

To prevent hearing damage while using headphones, go to **Settings** > **Sounds**, then tap the **Reduce Lound Sounds** button. On the following screen, you can set a maximum decibel limit, with 85 being the recommended amount.

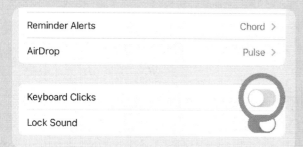

Turn off keyboard clicks

Your iPad will automatically emit a keyboard click sound every time you press a key on the on-screen keyboard. You can disable this by toggling the **Keyboard Clicks** switch at the bottom of the **Sounds** panel.

Prevent an app from tracking your location

Many apps will track your location as you go from place to place. Often this can be helpful, such as when you're using the Maps app to find your way around; but other apps, such as Facebook, might use your location to offer personalised adverts.

To prevent an app from tracking your location, open the **Settings** app then scroll down until you see it in the big list of apps installed on your iPad. Tap on the app, select **Location**, then decide how the app can track you using the four options at the top of the screen.

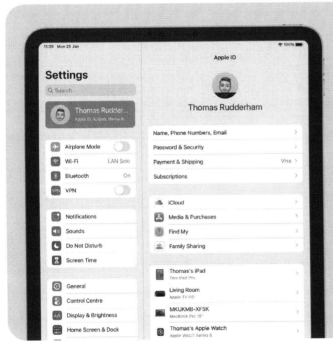

Update your Apple ID

Think of your Apple ID like a passport to everything Apple-related. Your Apple ID includes not only your personal information, but your payment settings, subscriptions, and access to other Apple devices like a Mac or iPhone.

Because your Apple ID is so important, it's a good idea to check it every now and then to make sure everything is up to date. To do this, open the **Settings** app, then tap on your **name and profile photo** at the top of the screen. On the following panel you'll be able to see all of your personal details and subscriptions in one place.

Use Screen Time to set limits

Discover how long you've spent using your iPad, and limit distractions...

If you're concerned or worried that you might be spending too long using your iPad, then the Screen Time panel included in the Settings app will help you work out exactly how long you've spent using apps, how many notifications you've received, or set time limits to prevent future distractions.

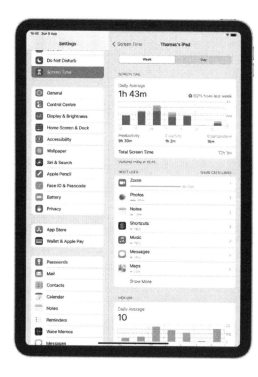

Find Screen Time

1 Open the **Settings** app, then tap on **Screen Time**.

2 Tap **See All Activity** at the top of the panel.

3 You can then view your Screen Time data for the current day or the last seven days.

As you'll see, the Screen Time panel is dense with information. You'll see total time spent with apps (some will be grouped into categories, such as "Productivity"), how many times you've picked up your iPad, and how many notifications you've received.

Downtime

Using the Screen Time settings panel it's possible to limit apps and notifications at a specific time, such as bedtime.

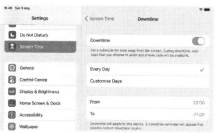

Set a Downtime schedule

Open the **Settings** app, tap on **Screen Time**, then choose **Downtime**. Toggle Downtime **on**, then use the **From** and **To** buttons to set a schedule.

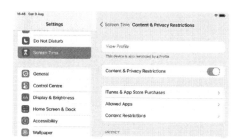

Block inappropriate content

If you would like to limit inappropriate content, such as R-rated films or adult websites, tap on **Content & Privacy Restrictions**, then toggle it on. On the following screen you'll find a massive number of restriction options.

View an activity report of your iPad usage

Using the Screen Time panel it's possible to view daily or weekly reports of your iPad usage. You can see how long you've spent using apps, how many notifications you've received, and even how many times you've picked up your iPad.

1 Open the **Settings** app, then tap on **Screen Time.** At the top of the panel you should see a brief report on your iPad usage. Tap **See All Activity** to see more...

2 On the following panel you'll see a brief overview of the total time spent on your device, broken down into categories.

3 Beneath is a panel called Most Used. It displays which apps you've used the most during the day or last week. Tap on an app to see a detailed breakdown.

4 Below the Most Used panel is the Pickups panel. It displays exactly how many times you've picked up your iPad, as well as the average amount of time passed between each pickup.

5 Further below is report panel of the notifications you've received. It's broken down by app, so you can see exactly which app is sending you the most notifications.

Other things you can restrict using Screen Time

By visiting the **Content & Privacy** panel in the Screen Time settings, you can limit a massive amount of content and features on a device, including:

- App installation
- Location Sharing
- Changes to passcodes
- Account changes
- Mobile data limits

- Volume limit
- Explicit language
- Screen recording
- Multiplayer games
- Explicit entertainment and books

See which apps are draining battery

Losing battery quickly? Here's how to see which apps are responsible...

The battery inside your iPad is massive, taking up most of its inside and being responsible for most of its weight. You'll typically get a days usage out of your iPad, but if you've noticed that the battery is draining quickly, then it's possible to see which apps are responsible. You can also work out how long you've spent using your iPad, and how long it has been asleep.

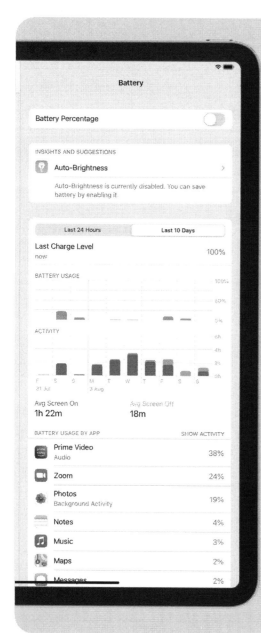

Take a glance at your battery

If you're worried that an app or service is using all your battery, then you can access a time chart which displays the battery level and activity over the last 24 hours, or 10 days. To do this:

1. Open the **Settings** app, then tap on **Battery**.

2. Scroll down and you'll find two charts covering your battery's charge level and activity.

3. You can toggle between the last 24 hours or 10 days using the blue tab above the charts.

4. Scroll down and you'll see a breakdown of which apps have used the most battery. Tap on one and you'll see the exact amount of time each app was used, and for how long it has been running in the background.

Show Battery Percentage

If your iPad is a little old and not lasting as long as it used to, go to **Settings** > **Battery**, then toggle **Battery Percentage** on. You'll now get a better idea of much battery power you have left.

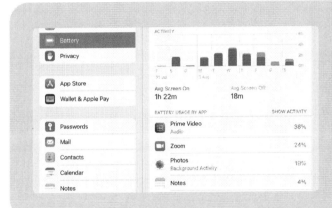

View battery usage by each app

From the **Settings** > **Battery** panel, scroll down and you'll see a list of all the apps you've used, and how much battery they've used up.

View more app usage

While looking at the app usage overview, tap on the **SHOW ACTIVITY** button and you'll see the exact time spent using each app.

Customise the Pointer

Make it easier to see the pointer, or adjust its scrolling speed...

If you're using a Magic Mouse, Magic Keyboard or Trackpad to control your iPad, then it's possible adjust how quickly the pointer moves across the screen, its size, and even it's overall contrast.

Adjust pointer scrolling speed

Open the **Settings** app, tap on **Accessibility**, then choose **Pointer Control**. Look for the **Scrolling Speed** slider, then adjust it to either increase or decrease the movement sensitivity.

Adjust the pointer size

To make the pointer circle larger or smaller, go to **Settings** > **Accessibility** > **Pointer Control**, then adjust the **Pointer Size** slider.

Disable pointer animations

With Pointer Animations enabled, the pointer morphs to match the shape of a hovered element, such as a button. If you'd rather it stay as a circular icon, go to **Settings** > **Accessibility** > **Pointer Control**, then toggle **Pointer Animations** off.

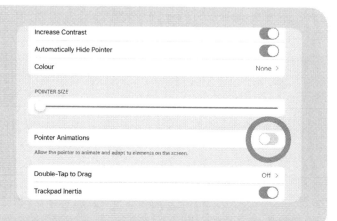

Customise Trackpad controls

Add additional features to your trackpad such as Tap to Click...

When you're using a trackpad with the iPad, such as a Magic Trackpad or the Magic Keyboard, a new panel is available in the Settings app. To find it open the Settings app and go to **General** > **Trackpad**...

Adjust trackpad scrolling speed

If you'd like to adjust the speed of the pointer when using a trackpad, go to **Settings** > **General** > **Trackpad**, then look for the **Tracking Speed** slider.

Enable Tap to Click

By enabling Tap to Click, it's possible to click on something by lightly tapping the trackpad with your finger. You'll find the Tap to Click option at **Settings** > **General** > **Trackpad**.

Enable Two-Finger Secondary Click

Toggle **Two-Finger Secondary Click** on, and you can easily initiate the long-press feature found throughout iPadOS by tapping with two fingers.

How to use Do Not Disturb

Prevent or limit interruptions and calls...

It can be rather annoying when a message, FaceTime call, or notification awakes you at night, or when your iPad lights up and emits a noise during an important meeting. These notifications can usually be overridden by simply muting your device or putting it into Airplane mode, but the Do Not Disturb feature is simpler and much more effective.

It works by completely silencing your iPad between a determined period of time, for example, midnight and 7 AM. During this time, your iPad won't make a noise or light up. You can, however, tell it to allow notifications and repeat calls to come through from specific contacts.

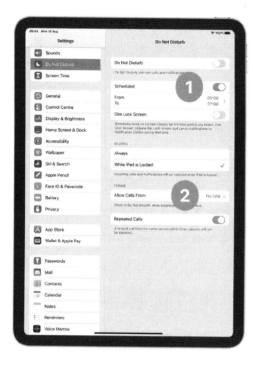

Explore Do Not Disturb

To activate or schedule Do Not Disturb, go to **Settings > Do Not Disturb**, then toggle it **on**. You can then...

1 **Schedule Do Not Disturb.** Use the **From** and **To** buttons to schedule Do Not Disturb, for example, when you go to bed.

2 **Enable important contacts.** If you're expecting an important call, or need to let certain contacts get in touch at all hours, then tap the **Allow Calls From** button. On the next panel you can let anyone call, no one at all, or those in your Favourites list (created within the Contacts app).

Enable Do Not Disturb

Swipe down from the top-right corner to access Control Centre, then tap the button near the top that looks like a crescent moon. This will enable Do Not Disturb, preventing any calls, messages or notifications from alerting you.

Activate for a period of time

To quickly activate Do Not Disturb for the next hour, until the morning, or until you leave your current location, **tap and hold** on the **Do Not Disturb** icon in Control Centre, then select an option.

Let repeat calls through

Toggle **Repeated Calls** on to let anyone bypass Do Not Disturb if they call more than once in a three-minute period. This might be helpful in emergency situations, or if there's something really important you should know about.

Siri settings

Adjust Siri's voice, language, and features...

Siri is a great digital assistant for asking questions, setting reminders, and sending messages, and it's highly customisable. By visiting the Siri & Search panel in the Settings app, you can change the voice and language, toggle "Hey Siri" on and off, announce messages out-loud and more.

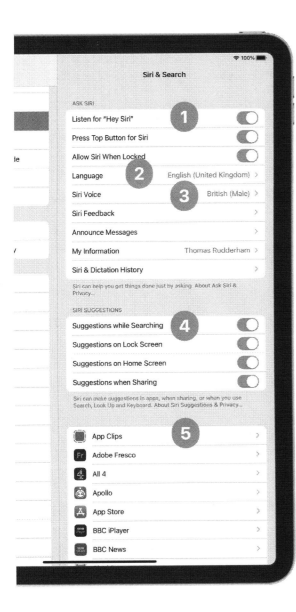

Explore Siri & Search

You can find all the Siri settings by going to **Settings > Siri & Search**...

1 **Listen for "Hey Siri".** When this is toggled on, you can activate Siri by saying "Hey Siri" out-loud near your iPad.

2 **Language.** Tap this option to choose from 20 different languages. For example, you can swap between English (United Kingdom), English (New Zealand), and English (India).

3 **Siri Voice.** This option lets you choose between male and female voices or localised accents.

4 **Siri Suggestions.** As you use your iPad, Siri will try to learn your habits by monitoring which apps you use and how you search your device. You can toggle these features on or off using these switches.

5 **App Suggestions.** As above, over time Siri learns how you use and interact with apps. You can switch off this feature for individual apps by selecting an app, then toggling off the switch called **Learn from this App**.

A guide to accessibility settings

Enable visual, audio, and physical accommodations...

Your iPad might be an intuitive device to use, but it's also packed with assistive features to help those with visual impairments or motor control limitations. You'll find the majority of them in the Accessibility panel within the Settings app. To get there, open **Settings**, tap **General**, then select **Accessibility**.

Enable button shapes

Buttons on your iPad usually look like a word or short piece of text. To make it more obvious which is a button and which is a piece of text, go to **Settings** > **Accessibility** > **Display & Text Size**, then toggle the **Button Shapes** switch **on**. This will display thin blue lines beneath buttons, and add small radio buttons to the inside of toggle switches.

Bold text

By bolding all text on your iPad, you can make it easier read small words and button. To do this, go to **Settings** > **Display & Brightness**, then toggle **Bold Text** on. Note that when this switch is toggled your iPad will need to be restarted.

Invert the colours of your screen

To flip the colours of your iPad's screen, go to **Settings** > **Accessibility** > **Display & Text Size**. You'll see two options: Smart Invert, and Classic Invert. Smart Invert will reverse the colour of everything except images, media and a limited number of apps. Classic Invert will reverse the colour of everything on the screen.

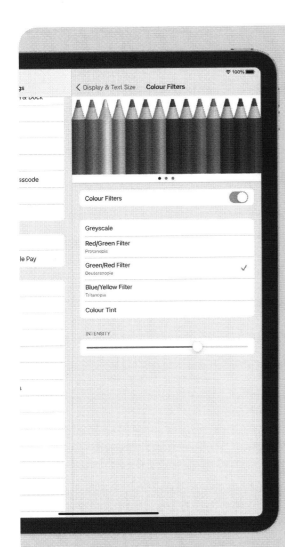

Adjust the display to accommodate for colour blindness

Colour blindness can be a hassle at the best of times in the real world, and it's a problem that remains when using your iPad to browse the web, examine photographs or generally interact with the user interface.

Thankfully a built-in accessibility feature can adjust the colour palette of the display to accommodate for colour blindness, making it possible to see tricky colours in a wide range of spectrums. Here's how it works:

1. Open the **Settings** app and go to **Accessibility** > **Display & Text Size** > **Colour Filters** then toggle **Colour Filters** on.

2. You'll see a preview of the effect in the graphic at the top of the screen (scroll it left to see two colour charts).

3. To fine tune the colour spectrum change, tap the filters below the image.

Enable subtitles

To enable subtitles and captions for entertainment on your iPad, go to **Settings** > **Accessibility** > **Subtitles & Captioning**, and toggle the top switch **on**.

After enabling subtitles, tap the **Style** button to choose from three preset styles. By tapping **Create New Style** you can also customise the font, size, colour, and background style.

Assistive Touch

Assistive Touch is a helpful feature for those with impaired physical and motor skills. It enables you to activate Multi-Touch features such as pinch-to-zoom with only one finger, or to trigger hardware buttons. To enable Assistive Touch, go to **Settings** > **Accessibility** > **Touch** > **Assistive Touch**, then toggle the button at the top of the screen.

With Assistive Touch enabled, you'll see a small square button appear on the side of the screen. By tapping this you can access a series of shortcut buttons which enable you to activate Notification Centre, Control Centre, Siri, functions on your iPad, return to the Home screen, or quickly access your favourite gestures.

Create an Assistive Touch gesture

If you'd like to mimic a Multi-Touch gesture (such as zoom) using Assistive Touch, then it's possible to do this by using a custom gesture. To create one, go to the Assistive Touch panel in the Settings app, then tap the **Create New Gesture** button. On the following screen, use two fingers to mimic zooming out of an image. Once you've done, tap **Save**. You can now use this gesture from the Assistive Touch panel by tapping the **Custom** button, indicated by a star.

Ask your iPad to read out-loud

Siri is great for setting reminders, opening apps, or finding out what's on at the cinema, but you can also use Siri to read out loud selected text, messages, and notes. This feature, called Speak Selection, is particularly useful for those with impaired eyesight.

To turn on Speak Selection go to **Settings** > **Accessibility** > **Spoken Content**, then toggle **Speak Selection**.

To speak words out loud, highlight any text (by double-tapping or tapping and holding on it), then tap the **Speak** button in the pop-up menu.

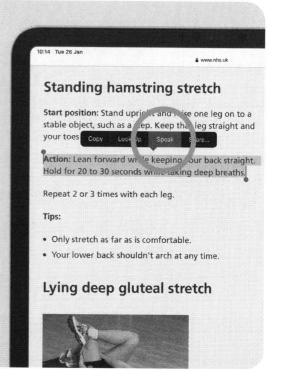

Connect a hearing aid

By connecting a hearing aid to your iPad you can experience higher-quality phone conversations. Go to **Settings > Accessibility > Hearing Devices**, where you can connect to any Bluetooth-enabled hearing aids. Any hearing aids with HAC compatibility (visit support. apple.com/kb/HT4526 to see a list of compatible devices) will also enable you to increase and decrease the volume independently for both ears, monitor battery usage and more.

Change the audio balance

If you're hard of hearing in one ear, or have a faulty pair of headphones, then it's possible to adjust the volume level in either the left or right channels. Go to **Settings > Accessibility > Audio/Visual**, then scroll down until you see a slide with L on the left side, and R on the right. Drag it left or right to adjust the volume. It might help to play music via the Music app while you make the adjustment.

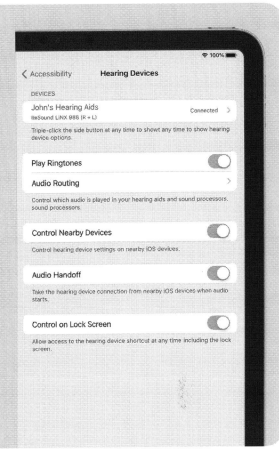

Use a magnifying glass

The iPad is designed to be easy for anyone to use, even those with visual impairments. However, there might be occasions where you need to zoom into the screen. Those with visual impairments might also appreciate the ability to get a closer look at things on the screen. Using a three-fingered Multi-Touch gesture, it's possible to display an on-screen magnifying glass, which you can move around to examine things in more detail. Here's how it works:

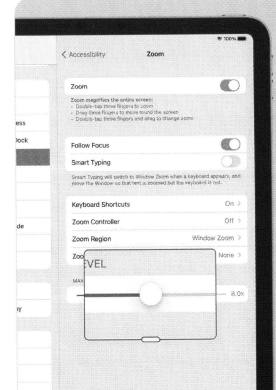

1 Go to **Settings > Accessibility**, then tap the **Zoom** option near the top of the screen.

2 You'll see a magnifying glass appear on-screen.

3 You can move the magnifying glass around by dragging the small button at the bottom of it.

4 You can hide the magnifying glass by tapping twice on the screen with three fingers.

What to do if you lose your iPad

First of all, don't panic!

It's probably somewhere obvious, like around the back of the sofa or in your backpack. If you've looked around and still can't find it then there are a few things you can try...

Call it using FaceTime

So long as your iPad isn't set to Silent Mode, then you can try giving it a call using FaceTime then listening out for the ringone alert. To do this:

1. Open FaceTime on an iPhone, Mac, or another iPad.

2. Tap the **plus** button, enter your own name or Apple ID, tap the blue link, then choose either **Audio** or **Video**.

3. Listen for the call as it comes through to your iPad.

Use Find My iPhone (for iPad)

Use another device or computer and go to www.icloud.com. Try to log in. If two-factor authentication is enabled and you're asked for a passcode, use your Mac or iPhone to get the code and enter it. If you don't have another iOS device or Mac, it's time to call Apple for further help.

Once you're logged into iCloud click the **Find iPhone** icon, then wait for your devices to load. Next, click on your **iPad** via the Map screen, or click the drop-down icon at the top of the screen and select it. In the pop-up panel, you'll be able to play a sound, erase your iPad, or place it into Lock Mode.

1 **Play Sound**
Click this button and your iPad will play a very loud alert sound. With luck you'll be able to quickly track its exact location.

2 **Lost Mode**
Click this button to immediately track your iPads location via the map screen. If Location Services are disabled on your iPad, then they will be temporarily activated to help you track its location. If your iPad is turned off, then Lost Mode will activate when it's next turned on.

3 **Erase iPad**
If the worst has happened and you don't think you'll be able to get your iPad back, then you can securely erase its contents to prevent someone from accessing your data. If your iPad is ever restored by someone else you can still track it and be assured that they can't unlock it without your Apple ID and password.

Other problems

How to quit troublesome apps, or even force your iPad to reboot...

It's rare, but sometimes hardware buttons stop responding or become stuck. Perhaps the Power button no longer clicks, or the volume buttons have stopped working. If your iPad has completely frozen and refuses to respond to taps or hardware buttons, then there are a few things you can try:

Force quit an app

If an app stops working:

If using a regular iPad:
Press the **Home** button twice to access the multitasking screen.

If using an iPad Pro:
Swipe up from the bottom of the screen, then stop halfway to access the same screen.

Next, slide the app which has stopped responding, up off the screen. This will force quit the app and remove it from the iPad's temporary memory.

Reboot your iPad

Sometimes your iPad might stop responding to touch. This is very rare, but it does happen from time-to-time. In these extreme cases, you can force the device to restart.

If using a regular iPad:
Press and hold both the **Home** and the **Power** buttons for around 10 seconds.

If using an iPad Pro:
Hold both the **Power** button and the **volume down** button for up to 10 seconds.

When the iPad restarts you can let go.

Let the battery run dry

In the unlikely event that the screen has stopped responding, *and* the buttons are stuck or broken, then let the battery run dry. Note that this might take up to 10 hours.

Wi-Fi problems

Wi-Fi connection problems can be a common occurrence. If you're experiencing regular disconnections or slow download speeds, then here are a few things to try:

- Reset the router. Turn it off, wait for 10 seconds to clear its cache, then power it back on.

- Get closer to the router. Thick concrete walls can sometimes block the connection.

- Reconnect. To do this go to Settings > Wi-Fi, tap on the network, choose Forget This Network, then try to reconnect to the same network.

iPad not charging

If your iPad isn't charging then there a couple of things you can try:

- Leave it plugged in. If the battery is fully drained, then it can take up to 20 minutes for it to start charging.

- Blow air into the charging port on the bottom of the iPad. Dust or pocket flint might have worked its way in over time. A can of compressed air is your best option.

Not powering on

If you've followed the previous step and left the iPad plugged in for at least 20 minutes, then something serious is likely to be happening. Your best bet is to make a Genius Bar appointment at your nearest Apple Store. Take the iPad in, explain the problem, then leave it to the experts.

Index A-M

Quickly find what you're looking for...

Index M-W

Quickly find what you're looking for...